ALSO BY PRATAP CHATTERJEE

Halliburton's Army: How a Well-Connected Texas Oil Company Revolutionized the Way America Makes War

Iraq, Inc.: A Profitable Occupation

ALSO BY KHALIL

Too Big to Fail

Zahra's Paradise (with Amir Soltani)

Mission Accomplished: Wicked Cartoons by America's Most Wanted Political Cartoonist

It Became Necessary to Destroy the Planet in Order to Save It

VERAX

VERAX

THE TRUE STORY OF WHISTLEBLOWERS, DRONE WARFARE, AND MASS SURVEILLANCE

PRATAP CHATTERJEE AND KHALIL

METROPOLITAN BOOKS
HENRY HOLT AND COMPANY NEW YORK

Metropolitan Books
Henry Holt and Company
Publishers since 1866
175 Fifth Avenue
New York, New York 10010
www.henryholt.com

Distributed in Canada by Raincoast Book Distribution Limited

AUTHORS' NOTE

This is a true story about real people, real events, and real issues of worldwide consequence. Primarily due to the artistic presentation or to protect our sources, some details have been changed, and the graphic illustration of a few of the characters and locations has been fictionalized. Certain time frames and the timing of certain actual quotations have also been moved, primarily for narrative fluency.

NOTE

The "lawful interception" industry sells data surveillance and analysis tools to law enforcement agencies like the police, the military, and theintelligence agencies. The clients must provide legal authorization to purchase these tools. The tools are often identical to those used by cyber-criminals and also by ethical hackers.

Library of Congress Cataloging-in-Publication data

ISBN: 9781627793551

First Edition 2017

Printed in the United States of America

10 9 8 7 6 5 4 3 2 1

VERAX

Prologue

SOMEWHERE IN CENTRAL ASIA
ZZZZBZZZZZZZZZZZZZZZZZZZZZ

ZZZZZZZZZZZZZZZZZZZZZZZZZZZZZZZZZZZZZZZZZZZZZZZZZZZZZZZZZZZZZZZZZZZZZZZZZZZZZZZZZZZZZZZZZZZZZZZZZZZZZZZ

zzzzzzzzzzzzzzZZ
ZZZZZZZzzzzzzz
zZZZZZZZZZZZZZZZZZZZZZZZZZ
WAAAAAA
WAAAAAAAAAAA
WAAAAA

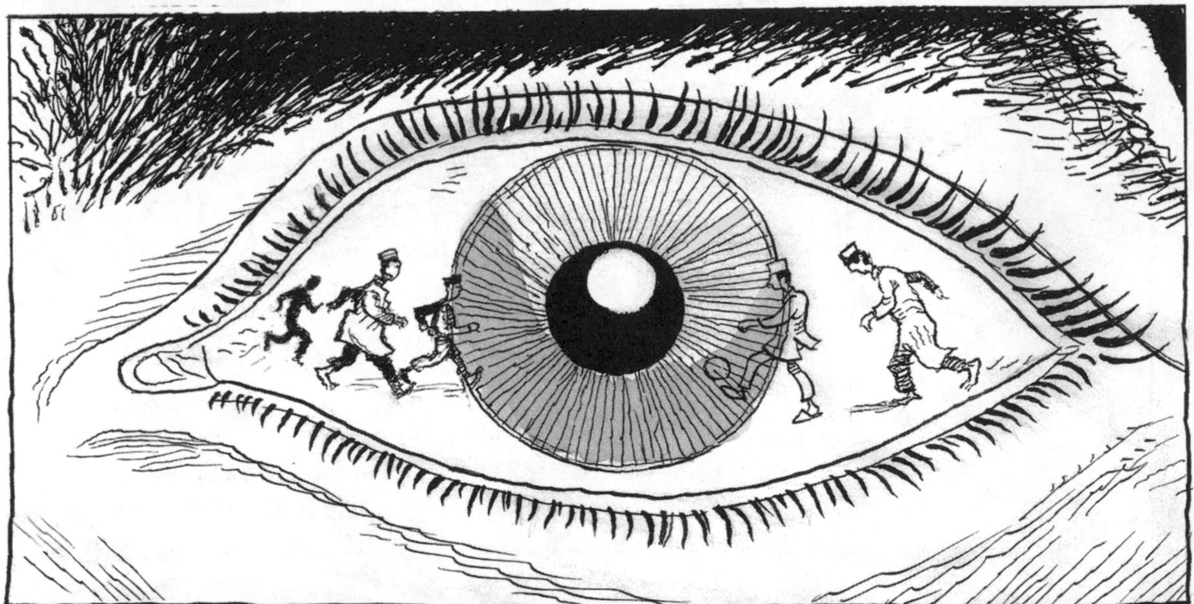

300°
147°
29°
N 36°
N 115°
GRG
LTHC
34/117
ARM

100°
-149
N 36°
N 115°
GRG
LTHC
34
ARM

35°
WAZIRISTAN

Chapter One

OCTOBER 2011

EDITOR IN CHIEF

KNOCK KNOCK

I KNEW IT WAS GOING TO BE A TOUGH SELL.

A FEW DAYS LATER, JULIAN ARRIVED AT OUR LONDON OFFICES WITH SEVERAL OTHER REPORTERS WHO WERE ALSO KEEN TO COLLABORATE WITH HIM.
WELCOME, EVERYBODY.
I'M JULIAN ASSANGE, WIKILEAKS, EDITOR IN CHIEF.
SARAH HARRISON, WIKILEAKS.
PRATAP CHATTERJEE, BUREAU OF INVESTIGATIVE JOURNALISM.
SARI HORWITZ, *WASHINGTON POST.*
LAURA POITRAS, FILMMAKER.
STEFANIA MAURIZI, *L'ESPRESSO.*
SOME OF YOU HAVE COME FROM NEW YORK AND WASHINGTON, OTHERS FROM ROME AND BERLIN.
YOU'VE ALL SEEN OUR LEAKED U.S. MILITARY CABLES FROM AFGHANISTAN AND IRAQ.
I PROMISE THAT YOU WILL NOT BE DISAPPOINTED WITH OUR LATEST SET OF DOCUMENTS.
BEFORE WE PROCEED, WE NEED YOU TO SIGN A NON-DISCLOSURE AGREEMENT FOR THESE DOCUMENTS.
AS ALWAYS, THIS IS INTENDED TO PROTECT YOU. EVERYONE WHO SIGNS THIS AGREES NOT TO REVEAL THESE DOCUMENTS BEFORE THE EMBARGO DATE.
WE HAVE ONE OF THESE FOR EACH OF YOU.
WHAT YOU WILL FIND IS BREATHTAKING. TOP-SECRET CLASSIFIED BRIEFINGS BY GOVERNMENT CONTRACTORS WHO ARE SELLING TECHNOLOGIES TO HACK INTO ANY PHONE AND ANY COMPUTER.
THESE COMPANIES ARE ABLE TO STORE OUR DATA FOR THE REST OF ETERNITY.
WE HAVE NAMED THIS PROJECT: THE ***SPY FILES!***

THIS SHADOWY WORLD OF SURVEILLANCE CONTRACTORS WAS RECENTLY THRUST INTO THE LIMELIGHT DURING THE ARAB SPRING. ON MARCH 5, 2011, AT THE EGYPTIAN MINISTRY OF THE INTERIOR IN CAIRO...
UNITED
AGAINST
ضد الظلم
INJUSTICE
THE PEOPLE DEMAND REMOVAL OF THE REGIME
الشعب يريد إسقاط النظام
الشعب
OUT
الثورة

...THE CROWD SWARMED PAST THE POLICE AND TOOK OVER THE BUILDING.
INSIDE, THEY UNCOVERED EVIDENCE OF THE MUBARAK REGIME'S REIGN OF TERROR: A PRISON CELL, A CACHE OF WEAPONS STAMPED "MADE-IN-USA" AND EVEN A CONCEALED LOVE NEST.
FLIPPING THROUGH FILES LABELLED "TOP SECRET," A DOCTOR BY THE NAME OF MUSTAFA HUSSEIN STUMBLED UPON A SUSPICIOUS ITEM.
GAMMA? WHAT IS THIS GAMMA?
GAMMA TECHNOLOGIES

GAMMA IS AN ANGLO-GERMAN SURVEILLANCE COMPANY. THEY SELL HACKING TECHNOLOGY TO REPRESSIVE REGIMES LIKE THE MUBARAK GOVERNMENT IN EGYPT.

HERE'S ONE CONTRACT FROM GAMMA.
Commercial offer: with offer dated 29 June 2010 to provide FinSpy software to SSI for 287,000 euros.
HERE'S ANOTHER ONE.
1 January 2011 comprehensive spying system in the location where targeted computer exists.

MUSTAFA HUSSEIN
WHAT DOES THIS EQUIPMENT DO?
IT'S CALLED A "TROJAN HORSE," A PIECE OF SOFTWARE YOU IMPLANT IN SOMEONE ELSE'S DEVICE.

AMR GHARBEIA FROM THE EGYPTIAN INITIATIVE FOR PERSONAL RIGHTS.
... TO CONTROL IT AND STEAL FROM IT. IT ALSO ENABLES IDENTITY FRAUD.

SO THAT'S HOW THE MUBARAK REGIME WAS TRACKING AND KEEPING A LID ON ANY AND ALL OPPOSITION.
THE FLIP SIDE OF THE INTERNET REVOLUTION.

HERE'S ANOTHER SURVEILLANCE COMPANY: AREA SPA OF ITALY.
THEY HAVE CONTRACTS WITH THE POLICE TO TAP PEOPLE'S PHONES.
THEY'VE ALSO BEEN WORKING WITH THE SYRIAN INTELLIGENCE TO INSTALL A MONITORING SYSTEM IN DAMASCUS.
WOW, SMALL WORLD!
AREA SPA WON A €13 MILLION CONTRACT IN SYRIA TO INSTALL EQUIPMENT FROM QOSMOS OF FRANCE AND UTIMACO FROM GERMANY.
DO WE HAVE ANY OF THEIR BROCHURES?
I THINK SO...
THERE!
Utimaco Competence in Lawful Interception
QOSMOS
Qosmos Boosting Monitoring Systems

Future

Lawful Interception for 10,000 to 50 million subscribers from 100 to 10,000 target

101001

Utimaco Safeware AG

LOOKS LIKE THEY CAN TRACK THE ENTIRE POPULATION OF SYRIA.

LOOK AT THIS!

Reliability:

Adequately decoding traffic even under unusual circumstances (e.g. non-standard protocol behavior)

Field-proven-based continuous feedback.

QOSMOS

LIKE ANY MAJOR INDUSTRY, THESE COMPANIES HAVE CONVENTIONS TO SELL THEIR PRODUCTS.
MANY OF THE COMPANIES WHOSE BROCHURES YOU JUST GOT ARE PLANNING TO ATTEND MILIPOL IN PARIS NEXT MONTH.
WHAT'S MILIPOL?
IT STANDS FOR MILITARY AND POLICE.
CONVENTION PARTICIPANTS ARE GOVERNMENT BUYERS FROM ALL OVER THE WORLD IN THE MARKET FOR GUNS, RIOT CONTROL EQUIPMENT, AND NOT LEAST — INTELLIGENCE GATHERING TOOLS.
WITH THE HELP OF THESE CLASSIFIED BRIEFINGS, YOU CAN CONFRONT THE COMPANIES DIRECTLY.
ALL WE ASK IS THAT YOU CREDIT WIKILEAKS IN YOUR REPORTING AS THE SOURCE OF THE MATERIAL.
WHERE DID YOU GET THESE DOCUMENTS?
THAT, AS ALWAYS, IS OUR TRADE SECRET!
WE WORK WITH WHISTLEBLOWERS WHO LEAK INFORMATION TO US IN THE PUBLIC INTEREST TO EXPOSE WRONGDOING BY POWERFUL FORCES SUCH AS NATIONAL GOVERNMENTS.
THESE DOCUMENTS ARE UPLOADED TO US ANONYMOUSLY. WE DON'T KNOW THE SOURCE OURSELVES.

TEN YEARS OF REPORTING ON THE WAR ON TERROR FROM BAGHDAD TO KABUL HAD TAUGHT ME THAT SPYING FOR NATIONAL SECURITY HAD BECOME A BOOMING BUSINESS.

AND I HAD LITTLE REASON TO DOUBT HIM. FROM THE FIRST TIME I EMAILED HIM BACK IN 2009, HE'S ALWAYS COME UP WITH ASTONISHING AND ACCURATE REVELATIONS.

LIKE THE CACHE OF MILITARY SECRETS WIKILEAKS PUBLISHED OVER THE PREVIOUS 15 MONTHS ON THE WARS IN AFGHANISTAN AND IRAQ...

AND PUT A BULL'S-EYE ON JULIAN'S BACK. EVERY WESTERN GOVERNMENT WANTED HIM SILENCED.

PARIS, WORLD CAPITAL FOR ALL THINGS GLAMOROUS: GASTRONOMY, HAUTE COUTURE, BEAUX ARTS ARCHITECTURE.
BUT GROUND ZERO FOR COMMAND AND CONTROL?
BEHOLD, THE CRÈME DE LA CRÈME OF THE GLOBAL MILITARY-POLICE-INTELLIGENCE-SURVEILLANCE COMPLEX HAWKING ITS WARES!
CHINA
INDIA
2G
2E
1H
1G
TASER
NAR
NICE
NW
MP SEC
ITALY
SURE
SOUTH
TASER
TEIJIN
TEIJIN
ARAMID
Vision
POLICE
Continuously working on better protection
TWARON
A.R.A.S.
POLICE

DEFEAT ENCRYPTION! DEPLOY A SECRET AGENT! TOTAL CONTROL OVER YOUR TARGETS!
WE CAN CAPTURE, PROCESS, AND ANALYZE ALL TYPES OF INFORMATION SENT OVER A WIDE SPECTRUM OF TELECOMMUNICATION NETWORKS.
CAN YOU LISTEN IN ON SKYPE CALLS?
OF COURSE!
OUR SOFTWARE CAN CAPTURE THE DATA TRAFFIC OF AN ENTIRE NATION!
WAS THE EAGLE SOFTWARE THAT AMESYS SOLD TO LIBYA USED TO SPY ON DISSIDENTS?
NO COMMENT.

A FEW DAYS AFTER I RETURNED TO LONDON:

SO, WHAT DO YOUR EDITORS THINK OF WHAT YOU SAW?

NEWSNIGHT AT THE BBC WANTS US TO DO A PIECE ON SOPHOS, A BRITISH COMPANY WHOSE SUBSIDIARY IS INVOLVED IN SYRIA.

THE *POST* WANTS A PIECE ON THE WIRETAPPERS' BALL, A TRADE SHOW FOR MAKERS OF SURVEILLANCE GEAR.

L'ESPRESSO WANTS AN ARTICLE ON THE HACKING TEAM OF ITALY.

Chapter Two

AFTER THE BRIEFING, I MET UP WITH FILMMAKER LAURA POITRAS.

I HOPE YOU DON'T MIND ME RECORDING YOU?

WHAT DO YOU PLAN TO DO WITH THIS FOOTAGE?

STATE SURVEILLANCE WILL BE THE THIRD PART OF MY TRILOGY ON THE "WAR ON TERROR."

WHAT WERE THE FIRST TWO ABOUT?

THE FIRST WAS ABOUT IRAQIS UNDER U.S. OCCUPATION.

THE SECOND WAS ABOUT A YEMENI MAN IMPRISONED IN GUANTÁNAMO BAY...

...THIS ONE WILL PROBABLY FEATURE SOME NATIONAL SECURITY AGENCY WHISTLEBLOWERS IN WASHINGTON D.C. I'VE BEEN INTERVIEWING.

DOES THE NSA ALSO USE TECHNOLOGY FROM GAMMA AND QOSMOS?

HA HA HA! ARE YOU KIDDING?

THAT'S CHILD'S PLAY COMPARED TO WHAT THEY CAN DO!

REALLY? LIKE WHAT?

HAVE YOU EVER HEARD OF *THIN THREAD*?

I FIRST LEARNED ABOUT THIN THREAD FROM FORMER NSA CRYPTOLOGISTS BILL BINNEY AND ED LOOMIS.
THEY INVITED ME TO THEIR FAVORITE DINER TO TALK ABOUT IT.
Double T Diner
IT WAS A TOOL FOR SPYING ON ANY DIGITAL ACTIVITY.
Double T Diner
DOUBLE "T" FOR THIN THREAD, GET IT?
HA HA!
BILL BINNEY HAD BEEN A CRYPTOLOGIST AT THE NSA FOR 36 YEARS.
IN THE LATE 1990S THERE WERE 2.5 BILLION PHONES IN THE WORLD AND 1.5 BILLION IP ADDRESSES.
THAT'S EQUAL TO ROUGHLY 20 TERABYTES OF INFORMATION PASSED AROUND THE WORLD EVERY MINUTE.
WE WERE FOCUSED ON TARGETS OF INTEREST AND ZONES OF SUSPICION AROUND THEM.
AS FOR ED LOOMIS, HE HAD BEEN AN NSA CRYPTOLOGIST FOR 37 YEARS.
WE LAID OUT A DESIGN THAT WE CALLED "THIN THREAD" THAT COULD TAKE RAW BITS, 1'S AND 0'S, AND TRANSFORM THEM INTO A CONTIGUOUS MESSAGE TO SEE IF ANY INTELLIGENCE COULD BE ACQUIRED FROM IT.
IMAGINE ALL THE DATA FROM PERSONAL FINANCIAL TRANSACTIONS, TRAVEL RECORDS, WEB SEARCHES, GPS EQUIPMENT, AND ANY OTHER ATTRIBUTES AN ANALYST MIGHT FIND USEFUL IN PINPOINTING "BAD GUYS."
THERE WAS CAPABILITY WHERE WE COULD DETECT WHETHER THE COMMUNICANT WAS A U.S. ENTITY OR NOT.
DID IT WORK?
WE GOT PERMISSION FROM THE GENERAL COUNSEL TO TEST IT. WE SET IT UP AT 18 FOREIGN SITES.
AND IT WORKED.

ON SEPTEMBER 14, 2001, I HAD A MEETING WITH THE GENERAL COUNSEL FOR OPERATIONS AND SEVERAL OTHER ATTORNEYS.

THE PURPOSE OF THIS TECHNOLOGY IS TO MONITOR WHAT PEOPLE ARE DOING. THE NSA DRAWS SOCIAL NETWORKS FOR EVERYBODY.
THINK OF A DOMAIN AS AN ACTIVITY SUCH AS PHONE CALLS OR BANKING.
THINK OF MAPPING ALL THAT DATA ON A GRAPH. YOU CAN PULL YOUR ENTIRE LIFE TOGETHER AND LOOK AT IT OVER TIME.
YOU INDEX ALL THE DATA TO THE GRAPH, YOU CAN PULL OUT A COMMUNITY AND THE OUTLINE OF THE LIFE OF EVERYBODY IN THAT COMMUNITY.
THE SOFTWARE, ONCE IT TAKES IN DATA, WILL BUILD PROFILES OF EVERYBODY IN THAT DATA.
AND THAT INVOLVES ANYBODY IN THE COUNTRY, EVEN SENATORS AND REPRESENTATIVES—ALL OF THEM! SINCE WE HAD TO PROTECT THEIR IDENTITIES, ACCORDING TO OUR LAWS AND THE PRIVACY RIGHTS OF U.S. CITIZENS, WE BUILT IN PROTECTIONS.
THIN THREAD ANONYMIZED U.S. ENTITIES, SO THAT THE NSA COULDN'T REALLY TELL WHO THEY WERE LOOKING AT.
UNFORTUNATELY, WHEN THE NSA CREATED STELLAR WIND AFTER 9/11, THEY TOOK AWAY THE CONTROLS THAT I CREATED AND TURNED IT ON **YOU** AND I'M SORRY FOR THAT!
THIS WAS SOMETHING THE STASI, THE KGB, OR THE GESTAPO WOULD HAVE **LOVED** TO HAVE HAD!
JUST BECAUSE WE'RE A DEMOCRACY DOESN'T MEAN WE WILL STAY THAT WAY.

BINNEY BELIEVED THAT STELLAR WIND WAS UNCONSTITUTIONAL BECAUSE THE NSA HAD REMOVED THE PRIVACY SAFEGUARDS.
SO HE TOOK HIS CONCERNS TO CONGRESS. BUT INSTEAD OF BEING A HERO, HE'S BEEN TREATED LIKE A CRIMINAL.
23
POLICE
POLICE
FBI
POLICE
THEY BURST INTO HIS HOUSE AND POINTED A GUN AT HIM.
FBI
FBI
TELL US SOMETHING THAT WILL IMPLICATE YOUR COLLEAGUES IN A CRIME!
FBI
I CAN TELL YOU ABOUT A CRIME.
FBI
FBI
GEORGE BUSH, DICK CHENEY, GEORGE TENET, AND MICHAEL HAYDEN HAVE CONSPIRED TO SUBVERT THE CONSTITUTION.
ARE YOU BEING FUNNY?
FBI
NOT AT ALL. THERE'S A HIGHLY CLASSIFIED PROGRAM CALLED STELLAR WIND TO CONDUCT DOMESTIC SPYING.
I'M TALKING ABOUT 20 TRILLION COMMUNICATIONS BY AMERICANS. THAT'S AN EXTREME, IMPEACHABLE CRIME.
FBI
FBI
FBI

WHO WERE THE OTHER PEOPLE THAT WERE RAIDED THAT DAY?

J. KIRK WIEBE, ED LOOMIS, AND DIANE ROARK.
WHO ARE THEY?

KIRK, LOOMIS, AND I WERE THE ONES WHO WENT TO CONGRESS. DIANE ROARK WAS THE SENIOR STAFFER ON THE SENATE INTELLIGENCE COMMITTEE.
SHE WAS THE ONE WHO WAS LOOKING INTO OUR COMPLAINT AGAINST THE NSA, TALKING ABOUT CORRUPTION, FRAUD, WASTE, AND ABUSE.

THEIR COMPLAINTS HAD COINCIDED WITH A *NEW YORK TIMES* EXPOSÉ OF WARRANTLESS WIRETAPPING.
SO WAS THE FBI LOOKING FOR THE SOURCE OF THE LEAKS?

THAT WAS THE PRETEXT, YES. WHAT THEY WERE REALLY DOING WAS RETRIBUTION AND INTIMIDATION.

THEY FABRICATED SEVERAL CHARGES AND ATTEMPTED TO INDICT US ON THEM.

FORTUNATELY, WE WERE ABLE TO PRODUCE EVIDENCE THAT WOULD MAKE THEM LOOK VERY SILLY IN COURT, SO THEY DIDN'T DO IT.

THE ONE MAN THEY CAUGHT WAS THOMAS DRAKE, WHO HAD TALKED TO THE MEDIA.

LAURA AND I CONTINUED THE CONVERSATION IN MY OFFICE.

IMAGINE FOR THE MOMENT HAVING YOUR VERY HOME RAIDED BY THE FBI...
IMAGINE HAVING YOUR FAMILY PICTURES, BOOKS, PERSONAL PAPERS, AND COMPUTERS SEIZED AND TAKEN AWAY.
FBI
IMAGINE THE GOVERNMENT DOING EVERYTHING TO ISOLATE YOU FROM YOUR FAMILY, YOUR FIVE SONS, YOUR FRIENDS, YOUR COLLEAGUES.
IMAGINE FINDING YOURSELF WITHOUT A JOB OR A FUTURE, AND THREATENED WITH THE PROSPECT OF LIFE IN PRISON.
IS THAT FREEDOM?
THE GOVERNMENT REGARDS ME AS AN ENEMY OF THE STATE.
PRESS .ORG
I HAVE FORMALLY RAISED GRAVE CONCERNS ABOUT GOVERNMENT WRONGDOING THROUGH PROPER CHANNELS.
WE NOW LIVE IN AN ORWELLIAN WORLD WHERE WHISTLE-BLOWING...
...IS EQUATED WITH...
...ESPIONAGE!

THE GOVERNMENT AGREED TO DROP THE CHARGES IF DRAKE PLEADED GUILTY TO A SINGLE COUNT OF MISUSING A GOVERNMENT COMPUTER.
THOMAS DRAKE'S TRIAL, BALTIMORE, JULY 15, 2011
CALLING THE CASE OF UNITED STATES VERSUS THOMAS ANDREWS DRAKE.
CRIMINAL NUMBER RDB10-0181, HERE FOR SENTENCING TODAY.
THERE WAS NO AGREEMENT AS TO THIS DEFENDANT'S CRIMINAL HISTORY AND HE HAS NONE AND HAS NO PRIOR CRIMINAL RECORD OF ANY KIND, NOT EVEN A PARKING TICKET.
IT'S NOT OFTEN I HAVE A DEFENDANT IN FRONT OF ME THAT HAS A BETTER RECORD THAN I DO.
BUT THAT WAS MY COLLEGE DAYS.
WHAT HE PLED GUILTY TO IS THEFT! HE STOLE INFORMATION FROM THE NSA.
WHAT HE DID WAS INTENTIONAL! THE DECISION TO BEGIN TO PROVIDE INFORMATION TO THE REPORTER WAS NOT TAKEN LIGHTLY.
HOWEVER, THE GOVERNMENT HAS DECIDED TO DROP ALL CHARGES AGAINST MR. DRAKE. BUT AT A MINIMUM, THE FINE OUGHT TO BE $50,000.
I FIND THAT UNCONSCIONABLE. UNCONSCIONABLE!
HOW MANY DEFENDANTS DO YOU THINK WAIT TWO AND A HALF YEARS AFTER THEIR HOME IS SEARCHED BEFORE AN INDICTMENT IS RETURNED?
I'LL ESTIMATE IT FOR YOU. NOT MANY. THIS DOESN'T PASS THE SMELL TEST.
THERE'S NOT GOING TO BE A FINE IN THIS CASE.
HE WAS HARASSED FOR YEARS! IS THAT THE CHANGE THAT OBAMA PROMISED US?

TWO MONTHS AFTER OUR TEAM OF JOURNALISTS MET IN LONDON, WE PUBLISHED OUR STORIES SIMULTANEOUSLY ON THE DAY THAT WIKILEAKS RELEASED THE SPY FILES AT A PRESS CONFERENCE.
CAN I BORROW YOUR PHONE, PRATAP? I DON'T OWN ONE.
I KNOW IT SOUNDS LIKE SOMETHING OUT OF A HOLLYWOOD B MOVIE, BUT AS OF TODAY, MASS INTERCEPTION SYSTEMS BUILT BY WESTERN CONTRACTORS FOR GOVERNMENTS TO SPY ON THEIR OWN POLITICAL OPPONENTS ARE NOW A REALITY.
TODAY, WIKILEAKS BEGAN RELEASING A DATABASE OF HUNDREDS OF DOCUMENTS FROM AS MANY AS 160 INTELLIGENCE CONTRACTORS IN THE MASS SURVEILLANCE. INDUSTRY.
WHO HERE HAS AN IPHONE?
WHO HERE HAS A BLACKBERRY?
AND WHO HERE USES GMAIL?
CONGRATULATIONS, YOU'RE ALL SCREWED!

Chapter Three

THE SPY FILES WERE COVERED BY DOZENS OF PAPERS AROUND THE WORLD, FROM THE *WASHINGTON POST* IN THE UNITED STATES TO THE HINDU IN INDIA. EMBOLDENED WITH THIS SUCCESS, I APPROACHED IAIN WITH A PROPOSAL TO INTERVIEW U.S. DRONE VICTIMS.

IN THE END, IAIN AGREED TO SPRING FOR HALF MY EXPENSES, ON THE CONDITION THAT I "DELIVER THE GOODS, THIS TIME."

I HAPPEN TO HAVE AN ART DEGREE FROM SAN FRANCISCO STATE UNIVERSITY, SO I USED THAT TO SLIP UNDER THE RADAR.

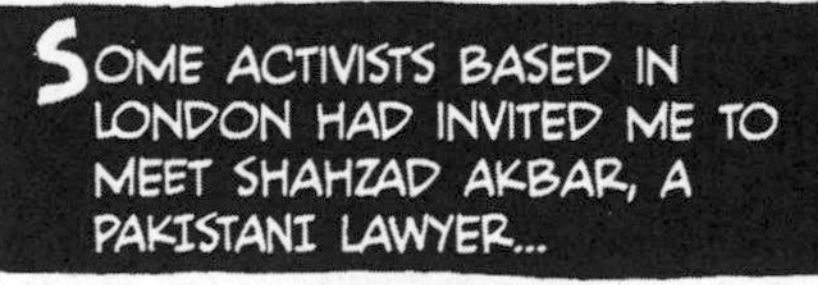

...WHO WAS CONVENING AN IMPORTANT JIRGA* TO DISCUSS DRONES.

AT ISLAMABAD'S FOUR-STAR MARGALA HOTEL

* PASHTUN FOR A TRIBAL ASSEMBLY OF ELDERS TO DISCUSS MAJOR EVENTS.

AT A WELCOMING MEAL, I WAS ASSIGNED TO A TABLE OF TEENAGE RELATIVES OF DRONE VICTIMS, WHO TOOK THE OPPORTUNITY TO QUIZ ME ON THEIR FAVORITE TOPIC.
WHERE YOU COME FROM, DO YOU WATCH SOCCER?
OF COURSE, I LOVE SOCCER!
DO YOU PLAY SOCCER?
YES, I PLAY MIDFIELD.
IN FACT, THEY CALL ME MARADONA!
HAHAHAHAHAHAHAHA!
WHAT'S YOUR FAVORITE TEAM?
ARSENAL, MY LOCAL TEAM.
WHAT DO YOU THINK OF MANCHESTER UNITED?
WHAT ABOUT BRAZIL?
THOSE ARE THE BEST!
WHAT ARE THE NAMES OF YOUR TEAMS?
I PLAY FOR BRAZIL...
...AND HE PLAYS FOR MANCHESTER UNITED.
HAHAHAHA HAHA!

OUTSIDE THE BALLROOM, A MAN WAS HOLDING PICTURES OF DEAD RELATIVES, WHILE INSIDE THE JIRGA WAS UNDERWAY.

* A LONDON-BASEFD ADVOCAY GROUP FIGHTING UNLAWFUL COUNTERINSURGENCY POLICIES.

THREE DAYS LATER, BACK AT THE OFFICE IN LONDON
HELLO? THIS IS PRATAP.
PRATAP? SHAHZAD AKBAR IN ISLAMABAD. LISTEN, DO YOU REMEMBER MEETING TARIQ AT THE MARGALA HOTEL?
TARIQ? ONE OF THE SOCCER-CRAZED TEENAGERS?
WE JUST HEARD HE WAS KILLED IN A DRONE STRIKE!
WHAT? THAT YOUNG KID?
WE ARE TRYING TO FIND PICTURES OF HIM, AND I THOUGHT YOU MIGHT HAVE TAKEN SOME.
I... I MIGHT HAVE A VIDEO OF HIM. I FILMED EVERYONE WHO CAME.
PRATAP, THAT WOULD BE REALLY HELPFUL. YOU THINK YOU CAN FIND IT?

COPY
Send
RING!
I THINK THAT IS TARIQ. I'LL SEND COPIES TO EVERYONE TO SEE IF THEY CAN CONFIRM IT.
RING!
WRONG BOY, PRATAP. THE TARIQ WHO WAS KILLED HAD A FUZZ OF A BEARD.
IS IT POSSIBLE THAT YOU HAVE IMAGES OF THE OTHER TARIQ?
HMM... LET ME CHECK. MAYBE.

CLICK
PAUSE
CLICK
CLICK
CLICK
CLICK
ZOOM
TAP
TAP
TAP
SEND
IS THIS THE CORRECT TARIQ, SHAHZAD?
YES, THIS IS THE BOY WHO WAS KILLED.
HE WAS JUST SIXTEEN.

IT'S ONE THING TO WRITE ABOUT VICTIMS AS A REPORTER...
...BUT QUITE ANOTHER TO EXPERIENCE THEIR DEATH AS A HUMAN BEING...
...UP CLOSE AND PERSONAL!
ZZZZZZZZZZZZZZZZZZZZZZZZZ

KICK!
GOOOOAAAL!
FFWOMMMMM
BLAM!
WOW!
JIHAD MEETS HELLFIRE!

Chapter Four

* DEFENSE INTELLIGENCE AGENCY.

I CAN'T KEEP PAYING FOR YOU TO BRING ME BACK SOFTWARE BROCHURES.
I DON'T *BELIEVE* THIS! THAT VIDEO OF TARIQ THAT I BROUGHT BACK FROM PAKISTAN WENT *VIRAL!*
THAT WAS A GOOD STORY BUT...
MY FOOTAGE WAS ON *ABC NEWS TONIGHT,* FOR HEAVEN'S SAKE!
THE *SUNDAY MAIL* WANTS TO DO A PIECE. I'VE EVEN BEEN GET-TING CALLS FROM TONJE SCHEI,
A FILM-MAKER IN NORWAY.
PRATAP, WE HAVE A WHOLE DRONE TEAM THAT TRACKS EVERY DRONE KILLING. SOFTWARE CONTRACTORS ARE NOT SEXY!
BUT THAT'S THE *CRUX* OF THE WHOLE DRONE WAR, IAIN, YOUR SMOKING GUN! DON'T YOU GET IT?
LOOK, PRATAP, I'M OVER BUDGET. I HAVE TO LAY YOU OFF.
IF YOU HAVE A GOOD STORY, I'LL LOOK AT IT.
BUT I'M **NOT** INTERESTED IN SOFTWARE BROCHURES ANYMORE!
AND I THOUGHT I WAS DOING SO WELL...

NOW WHAT?
I KNOW: I'LL CALL THE *GUARDIAN*. THEY LIKE MY WORK.
MATT SEATON, OPINION SECTION.

HI, MATT, I WAS WONDERING IF YOU MIGHT BE INTERESTED IN A STORY ABOUT A TEENAGER I MET IN PAKISTAN WHO WAS JUST KILLED BY THE CIA.

SOUNDS LIKE AN IMPORTANT STORY, PRATAP.

NOW THE CIA.
PRESS OFFICE.

HI, I'M WRITING AN ARTICLE ABOUT A TEENAGE BOY WHO WAS KILLED BY A CIA DRONE STRIKE IN PAKISTAN. CAN YOU COMMENT?

WHO ARE YOU WRITING THIS FOR, IF I MAY ASK?
THE *GUARDIAN* IN THE UK.

OK, WE'LL GET BACK TO YOU.

BUT I MUST WARN YOU...
...WE DON'T REALLY COMMENT ON THESE MATTERS.

OF COURSE THE CIA NEVER GOT BACK TO ME. BUT MATT RAN MY ARTICLE IN THE GUARDIAN'S WEB SITE.

theguardian
Drones (military) Opinion
The CIA's unaccountable drone war claims another casualty
Pratap Chatterjee
If Tariq Aziz, the 16-year old soccer fan I met was a 'terrorist' let the CIA prove

RING!

GOOD PIECE, PRATAP. THANK YOU FOR TELLING THE WORLD ABOUT WHAT HAPPENED TO TARIQ.

I JUST SENT YOU A DVD OF TARIQ'S FUNERAL. YOU CAN PICK IT UP AT CLIVE'S OFFICE AT REPRIEVE.

I WENT THERE RIGHT AWAY,

AND PLAYED THE DVD.

WHY WAS TARIQ KILLED? I HAD TO GET TO THE BOTTOM OF THIS..

WAS IT POSSIBLE THAT THE MUCH-VAUNTED PRECISION TARGETING IN THE DRONE WAR WAS NOT AS RELIABLE AS CLAIMED?
I'D HEARD THAT SOME PEOPLE WERE QUESTION-ING THE ACCURACY OF DRONE STRIKES.
ONE OF THEM WAS KATE CLARK OF THE AFGHANISTAN ANALYSTS NETWORK.
...U.S. SPECIAL FORCES ASSERT THAT THEY KILLED TALIBAN DEPUTY GOVERNOR OF TAKHAR, MUHAMMAD AMIN, IN AN AIR ATTACK ON SEPT-EMBER 2, 2010.
AND WAS IT REALLY MUHAMMAD AMIN?
NO, THE REAL MULLAH AMIN WAS LOCATED AND INTERVIEWED BY MICHAEL SEMPLE OF HARVARD.
THE MAN WHO WAS ACTUALLY KILLED WAS ZABET AMANULLAH.
KATE HAD INTERVIEWED ZABET AFTER HE WAS DETAINED AND BADLY TORTURED IN PAKISTAN. SHE WAS SURE THAT HE WAS NOT FIGHTING IN THE AFGHAN INSURGENCY.
HOW COULD THEY GET THEIR TARGETING SO WRONG?
AFTER INTERVIEWING DOZENS OF WITNESSES AS WELL AS THE U.S. SPECIAL OPERATIONS FORCES...
...IT BECAME CLEAR THAT INTELLIGENCE ANALYSTS HAD MIXED UP ZABET AMANULLAH'S MOBILE PHONE WITH THAT OF MULLAH AMIN.
THANKS. THAT'S MORE EVIDENCE THAT THE TECHNOLOGY ISN'T AS INFALLIBLE AS POLITICIANS CLAIM.

* STANDARD OPERATING PROCEDURES

BACK TO THE GUARDIAN.
MATT, NEITHER THE CIA NOR THE AIR FORCE IS GOING TO LEVEL WITH ME AND TELL ME HOW THEY CHOOSE TARGETS...
...LET ALONE HOW THEY MAKE MISTAKES.
SO, I WAS WONDERING IF YOU'D BE WILLING TO LET ME ATTEND AN INTELLIGENCE SOFTWARE CONFERENCE IN DENVER?
IF YOU PAY YOUR OWN EXPENSES.
FORTY-EIGHT HOURS LATER I WAS IN DENVER.
IF I GET A GOOD STORY, WILL YOU PUBLISH IT?
BUDGET OR NO BUDGET, PEOPLE WERE BEGINNING TO PAY ATTENTION TO MY STORIES IN THE GUARDIAN.
D-DIIS Worldwide CONFERENCE
OF COURSE, THE GUARDIAN ALWAYS WELCOMES GREAT JOURNALISM.
I WAS BACK ON THE TRAIL OF THE MILITARY-SURVEILLANCE-INDUSTRIAL COMPLEX.

AT THE DIA CONFERENCE, SOLDIERS AND CONTRACTORS MINGLED EASILY, TESTING OUT THE LATEST TECHNOLOGY.
WOULD IT BE POSSIBLE TO GET A DEMO OF HOW YOU USE SURVEILLANCE TO TRACK TERRORISTS?
YES, SIR. WE HAVE ONGOING DEMOS OF DCGS.
WHAT'S THAT?
THE DISTRIBUTED COMMON GROUND SYSTEM. IT'S THE COMPUTER NETWORK FOR THE INTELLIGENCE COMMUNITY.
THERE'S A VIDEO...
DCGSXA
DCGS'S MISSION IS TO COLLECT AND PROCESS VAST AMOUNTS OF INTELLIGENCE...
...IMAGERY FROM MANNED AND UNMANNED RECONNAISSANCE SOURCES.
HI. MY NAME IS STAFF SERGEANT PAUL JAMES. I WAS DEPLOYED IN KANDAHAR, AFGHANISTAN.
JAMES
MY TEAM AND I USED DCGS TO BUILD A DIGITAL SITUATIONAL TEMPLATE...
...WHICH ALLOWED US TO PINPOINT WHERE OPPOSITION ELEMENTS WERE STAGING THEIR MAIN EFFORTS.
ULTIMATELY THE SYSTEM ALLOWED A PLATOON-SIZED UNIT OF 14 SOLDIERS TO ACCOMPLISH WHAT A DIVISION OR LARGE COMPANY COULD DO.
THIS WAS A PROMISING FIRST CLUE INTO WHERE I MIGHT DISCOVER THE SOURCE OF THE FLAWS IN DRONE STRIKES.
DCGSXA
4:19/5:16

Chapter Five

THE PIECES OF THE PUZZLE CONNECTING SURVEILLANCE TO DRONES WERE BEGINNING TO FIT TOGETHER.
IF THE MILITARY RELIES ON DCGS TO TRACK PEOPLE, I NEEDED TO FIND OUT MORE ABOUT HOW IT DOES OR DOESN'T WORK.
OF COURSE, THERE'S NO WAY THAT THE MILITARY WOULD GIVE A REPORTER ACCESS TO THE ACTUAL SOFTWARE.
CONVENTION CENTER
WHO ELSE MIGHT BE WILLING TO TALK TO ME, EVEN OFF THE RECORD, ABOUT THE POSSIBLE FLAWS IN THIS SYSTEM?
I KNOW WHO I COULD ASK: LAURA POITRAS! AFTER ALL, SHE KNOWS WHISTLE-BLOWERS WHO WORK ON MILITARY SOFTWARE.

AFTER I RETURNED HOME TO LONDON, I GAVE LAURA A CALL.
HEY LAURA, DO YOU HAVE A MOMENT?
WHAT'S UP, PRATAP?
I THOUGHT I'D CHECK IN WITH YOU.
I'VE BEEN TRYING TO CONNECT THE DOTS BETWEEN THE NSA'S MASS SURVEILLANCE SYSTEM AND THE CIA'S DRONE WAR.
I'M SORRY, PRATAP, BUT I CAN'T TALK ABOUT THAT ON THE PHONE. I THINK I'M ON A WATCH LIST.
WHAT?
I DON'T WANT TO SOUND PARANOID, BUT MY LIFE HAS BEEN TURNED UPSIDE DOWN.
EVERY TIME I FLY TO EUROPE, IMMIGRATION OFFICERS HARASS ME AND TAKE AWAY MY EQUIPMENT.
BUT THAT'S CRAZY! HOW WILL YOU BE ABLE TO MEET WHISTLEBLOWERS LIKE BINNEY AND DRAKE?
HOW LONG HAS THIS BEEN GOING ON?
FIVE YEARS NOW.

LAURA TOLD ME THAT SHE HAD BEEN STOPPED ON FORTY OCCASIONS – PRETTY MUCH EVERY TIME SHE CAUGHT AN INTERNATIONAL FLIGHT.
JULY 2006
FLUGHAFEN WIEN
VIENNA INTERNATIONAL AIR
LAURA POITRAS, PLEASE REPORT TO THE SECURITY DESK!
SECU
POLIZEI
POLIZEI
POLIZEI
WHY WERE YOU IN SARAJEVO?

I'M A JOURNALIST. I WAS SHOWING MY FILM *MY COUNTRY, MY COUNTRY* ABOUT THE IRAQ WAR...
WHY ARE YOU SEARCHING MY LUGGAGE?
POLIZEI
YOU'RE FLAGGED. YOU HAVE A THREAT SCORE THAT IS OFF THE RICHTER SCALE.
POLIZEI
YOU'RE AT 400 OUT OF 400.
IS THIS A EURO-PEAN SCORING SYSTEM?
OR AN AMERICAN SYSTEM?
THIS IS YOUR GOVERNMENT'S SYSTEM. THEY'RE THE THE ONES ASKING US TO STOP YOU.
YOU'RE FREE TO GO. YOU CAN TAKE YOUR FLIGHT TO NEW YORK.
HOURS LATER, JFK AIRPORT, NEW YORK
UNITED
HSBC
UNITED
ALLIED AVIATION
LAURA POITRAS? PLEASE COME WITH US...
WELC
TO NEW Y
?

* SSSS: SECONDARY SECURITY SCREENING SELECTION
JFK INTERNATIONAL AIRPORT, NOV. 2010
I DO NOT CONSENT TO THIS SEARCH OR TO ANSWER YOUR QUESTIONS. I'M A JOURNALIST. MY WORK IS PROTECTED!
YOU KNOW, WE FIND IT A BIT SUSPICIOUS THAT YOU'RE NOT WILLING TO HELP YOUR COUNTRY BY ANSWERING OUR QUESTIONS.
IF YOU DON'T ANSWER OUR QUESTIONS, WE'LL FIND OUR ANSWERS ON YOUR ELECTRONICS.
LIBERTY INTERNATIONAL Airport, April 5, 2012
WHO DID YOU MEET IN THE UK? WHERE DID YOU GO?
YOUR OFFICERS HAVE ASKED ME THE SAME QUESTIONS ON MORE THAN FORTY OCCASIONS.
HOW MANY TIMES DO I HAVE TO EXPLAIN THAT I'M A FILMMAKER AND A JOURNALIST?
MY COUNTRY
by LAURA POITRAS
EMMY AWARDS NOMINEE
THE GEORGE POLK AWARD
PEABODY AWARDS LAURA POITRAS
Pulitzer Prize 2014
S×SW FILM FESTIVAL
BERLIN FILM FESTIVAL
WINNER INSPIRATION AWARD FULL FRAME FILM FESTIVAL
OSCAR NOMINATION 2014

I WANT YOUR NAME AND YOUR RANK.
MA'AM, IF YOU DON'T ANSWER OUR QUESTIONS, WE WILL CHARGE YOU WITH REFUSING TO COOPERATE WITH AN INVESTIGATION.
MA'AM, IF YOU DON'T STOP TAKING NOTES...
...I WILL HAVE TO HANDCUFF YOU. PUT AWAY YOUR PEN!
U.S. CUSTOMS AND BORDER PROTECTION
OFFICER
I'M SORRY, BUT I'M A JOURNALIST. AND I HAVE A RIGHT TO TAKE NOTES.
MA'AM, PUT AWAY YOUR PEN!
WHY CAN'T I USE A PEN?
BECAUSE IT COULD BE USED AS A WEAPON.
WELL, COULD I HAVE A CRAYON?
NO!
I'VE HAD IT.
I'M MOVING TO BERLIN!

SO HOW DO YOU DEAL WITH THIS NONSENSE? IS THERE ANY RECOURSE?
I'VE DECIDED THE ONLY WAY IS TO GO PUBLIC.
I'VE BEEN TALKING TO GLENN GREENWALD OF SALON.COM.
SMART MOVE, LAURA.
AND FOR NOW, THE ONLY WAY THAT I CHAT WITH MY SOURCES IS VIA FAILSAFE EN-CRYPTED SYSTEMS.
HMMM, I'VE TRIED TO USE ENCRYPTED EMAIL LIKE PGP BUT I HAVE TO CONFESS, I'M A DUD AT IT.
ALTHOUGH I DO KNOW HOW TO USE ENCRYPTED CHAT. THAT'S THE WAY I TALK TO WIKI-LEAKS.
OK, THEN, LET'S TALK VIA JABBER AFTER I'M DONE WITH EDITING THIS FOOTAGE.
GOOD LUCK! THE DRONE WORK IS IMPORTANT. YOU MUST KEEP IT UP.
WILL YOU USE ANY OF THE MATERIAL FROM OUR MEETINGS IN LONDON?
I HOPE SO, PRATAP, BUT TO BE HONEST, I'VE GOT SO MUCH MATERIAL.
NO WORRIES. I'LL REACH OUT TO GLENN, TOO.
DRONES AND SURVEILLANCE ARE RIGHT UP HIS ALLEY.

A FEW MONTHS LATER, LAURA DECIDED THAT SHE NEEDED TO TELL THE WORLD ABOUT THE STRUGGLE OF THE NSA'S WHISTLEBLOWERS.

LATER, OTHER REPORTERS WOULD ASK LAURA WHY SHE HAD PURSUED BINNEY'S STORY.

I FELT THE STORY COULDN'T WAIT FOR ME TO FINISH THE LONGER FILM, SO I APPROACHED THE *NEW YORK TIMES* TO MAKE A SHORT OP-DOC.*

HER VIDEO REACHED AN UNEXPECTED VIEWER IN HONOLULU.

**VIDEO OPINION PIECE*

IN EARLY 2013, JUST AS LAURA GOT DOWN TO WORK IN BERLIN TO EDIT HER FOOTAGE AND INTERVIEWS ON SURVEILLANCE, AN UNSOLICITED MESSAGE ARRIVED.

I know you've been harrassed. you don't like how this system works. I think you can tell this story.

Your victimization by the NSA system means that you are well aware of the threat that unrestricted, secret abilities pose for democracies.

Billions of U.S. communications are being intercepted. This I can prove. If you reveal this, heart attacks will be had over this.

I've only ever heard of Stellar Wind. Either you are taking huge risks, or you are trying to entrap me and the people I know, or you're crazy.

Have you seen the government files on me? Can you tell me why I'm being harassed? Why do they constantly ask me questions?

I haven't seen your files.

And I'm not going to ask you anything. I'm just going to tell you things. But I do ask one thing of you.

I want you to safely return this information to the American public so they can decide the kind of government that they want to live under.

I don't know if you are legit, crazy, or trying to entrap me. But don't worry, I will work with you. And I will protect your anonymity.

No, I fully intend to claim responsibility for my actions.

I plan to outline my motives and the dangers that I see inside the agency.

You cannot protect my identity. I don't want you to. I hope you will paint a target on my back.

Chapter Six

MEANWHILE, CONTINUING MY UPHILL STRUGGLE TO GET FUNDING TO INVESTIGATE DRONES AND SURVEILLANCE, I DECIDED TO LOOK FURTHER AFIELD.
I'M TRYING TO REACH KHALIL BENDIB. IS THIS STILL HIS PHONE NUMBER BY ANY CHANCE?
HEY, PRATAP, YES, THIS IS KHALIL, STILL CARTOONING AFTER ALL THESE YEARS. WHAT ABOUT YOU?
I'M TRYING TO FIND A MAGAZINE OR NEWSPAPER THAT WOULD BE INTERESTED IN MY RESEARCH INTO THE INTELLIGENCE AGENCIES.
WHAT HAVE YOU GOT? NEWSPAPERS LOVE TO SPILL SECRETS AND THEY LOVE A GOOD SCANDAL.
THIS IS ABOUT HOW THEY ROUTINELY SPY ON INNOCENT PEOPLE.
COULD MAKE A GOOD BOOK OR EVEN POLITICAL CARTOONS. ME, I'VE BEEN WORKING ON GRAPHIC NOVELS.
AND HAVE YOU HAD ANY LUCK WITH THEM?
MY FIRST ONE, ZAHRA'S PARADISE, WHICH IS ABOUT IRAN'S GREEN REVOLUTION IN 2009, HAS BEEN PUBLISHED IN SIXTEEN LANGUAGES SO FAR.
ZAHRA'S PARADISE
Amir & Khalil
WOW! GOOD FOR YOU!
ME, I'M OUT OF A JOB. LIKE MOST JOURNALISTS THESE DAYS.
MMM... I HEAR THAT YOUR OLD EMPLOYER, CORPWATCH, HAS LOST MOST OF ITS STAFF. PERHAPS YOU SHOULD GIVE THEM A CALL?
THAT'S AN IDEA... MAYBE THEY WILL EVEN GIVE ME MY OLD JOB BACK.

I CALLED JOSH KARLINER, THE FOUNDER OF CORPWATCH.ORG.

WE'VE LAID OFF THE STAFF AND SHUT THE OFFICE. THE ONLY WAY WE COULD AFFORD TO HIRE YOU IS IF YOU COULD RAISE THE MONEY.

CORPWATCH AGREED TO HIRE ME BACK.
I HAD MIXED FEELINGS ABOUT LEAVING LONDON.
BOTH THE BUREAU AND REPRIEVE, TWO KEY CRITICS OF THE DRONE WAR, WERE BASED HERE.
BUT I REALIZED THAT IF I WANTED TO WORK ON DRONE CONTRACTORS, I PROBABLY NEEDED TO GO BACK TO THE UNITED STATES.

MEANWHILE, HALFWAY ACROSS THE WORLD, LAURA'S TALE OF HARASSMENT HAD STRUCK A CHORD WITH JOURNALIST GLENN GREENWALD.

GLENN GREENWALD, WHO LIVED IN BRAZIL, HAD WRITTEN EXTENSIVELY ABOUT NATIONAL SECURITY EXCESSES.

GLENN'S SHARP POLITICAL ANALYSIS MADE HIM A POPULAR WRITER TO MANY, MYSELF INCLUDED. I KNEW THAT HE WAS INUNDATED, SO I WASN'T SURPRISED THAT HE DIDN'T RESPOND ABOUT MY DRONE WORK.

IN DECEMBER 2012, HE RECEIVED AN EMAIL FROM AN UNKNOWN SENDER, CALLING HIMSELF CINCINNATUS.
Beep
email

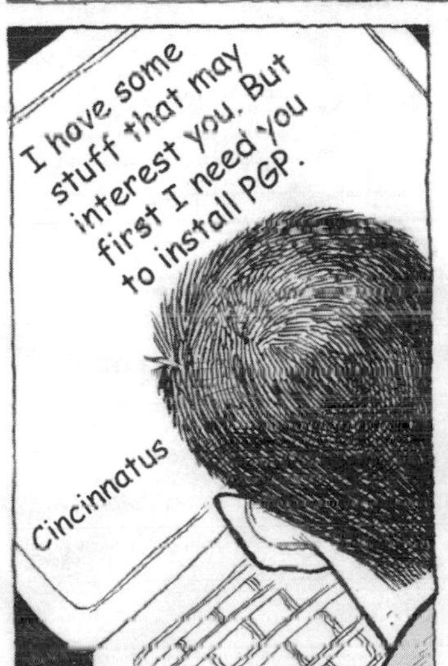
I have some stuff that may interest you. But first I need you to install PGP.
Cincinnatus

Who are you?

I am a senior member of the intelligence community. If you install PGP, we can chat.

Encryption matters, and it is not just for spies and philanderers.
Cincinnatus
Delete

The New York Times
GUNMAN MASSACRES 20 CHILDREN AT SCHOOL IN CONNECTICUT: 28 DEAD. INCLUDING KILLER
SANDY HOOK SCHOOL 1956

A FEW DAYS LATER.
So, have you done it?
Cryptographically Yours, Cincinnatus

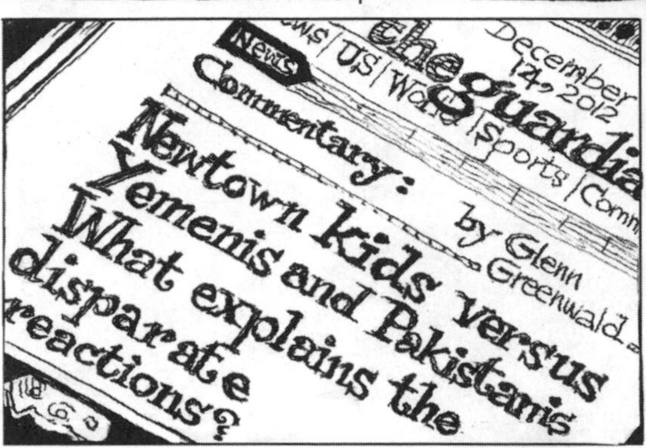

POINTING OUT WASHINGTON'S DOUBLE STANDARDS KEPT GLENN BUSY. TOO BUSY IN FACT.

WHILE SOME OF US UNSUCCESSFULLY STRUGGLED TO REACH GLENN, LAURA WAS LUCKIER.

WOULD YOU LIKE TO COME TO MY HOTEL TOMORROW? I'M STAYING AT THE MARRIOTT IN YONKERS.

LAURA TOLD ME SHE KNEW HOW CARELESS MOST JOURNALISTS WERE ABOUT PERSONAL SECURITY.

A FEW MINUTES LATER.

LAURA HAD STAYED IN TOUCH WITH THE MYSTERIOUS SOURCE AND VERIFIED HIS CLAIMS WITH THE HELP OF JAKE APPELBAUM, A SECURITY RESEARCHER.

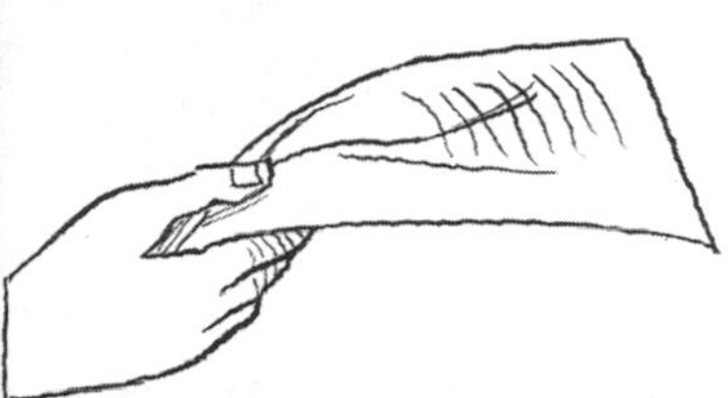

"NSA DIRECTOR KEITH ALEXANDER LIED TO CONGRESS, WHICH I CAN PROVE."

"BILLIONS OF COMMUNICATIONS ARE BEING INTERCEPTED. THIS I CAN PROVE."

"IF YOU REVEAL THIS, HEART ATTACKS WILL BE HAD."

"I WANT YOU TO SAFELY RETURN THIS INFORMATION TO THE AMERICAN PUBLIC SO THEY CAN DECIDE THE KIND OF GOVERNMENT THAT THEY WANT TO LIVE UNDER."

NOW GLENN NEEDED TO INSTALL PGP TO COMMUNICATE WITH LAURA AND READ THE MATERIAL FROM HER SOURCE. BUT HE STILL COULDN'T FIGURE OUT HOW TO DO IT. FINALLY MICAH LEE OF THE ELECTRONIC FRONTIER FOUNDATION OFFERED TO HELP OUT.
MAY 13, 2013
HE PUT A COPY OF THE SOFTWARE ON A DRIVE AND DROPPED IT OFF AT THE FEDERAL EXPRESS OFFICE IN BERKELEY.
FedEx Office
SCREECH!
HI, I'M EXPECTING A PACKAGE. MY NAME IS GLENN GREENWALD. HAS IT ARRIVED YET?
YES, WE HAVE IT.
BUT IT IS BEING HELD IN CUSTOMS...
...FOR UNKNOWN REASONS.
MAY
MAY 15
MAY 16
MAY 17
MAY 18
MAY 19
MAY 19
FedEx
RRRIP
How to install PGP
?
All I got was some software. How do I even know that your source is real?
If you install PGP, you can talk to him yourself.
?
BEEP!
email
Your destination is HONG KONG

GLENN AND THE MYSTERIOUS SOURCE BEGAN TO TALK DIRECTLY.

I'VE ALSO BEEN TALKING TO THE *WASHINGTON POST* ABOUT THIS INFORMATION.

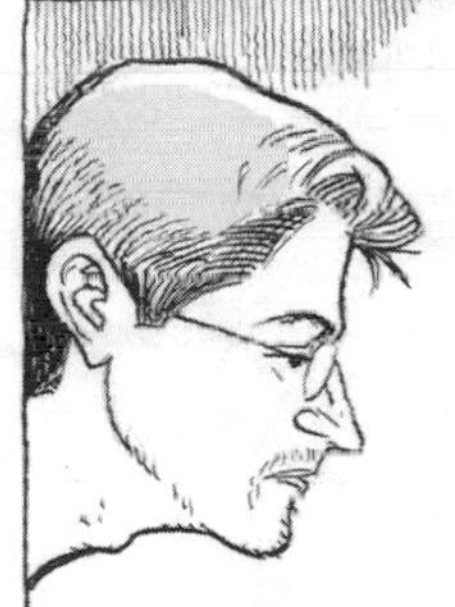

I WILL MEET YOU THERE AND GIVE YOU THE DOCUMENTS... I HOPE TO SPARK A WORLDWIDE DEBATE ABOUT PRIVACY AND INTERNET FREEDOM...

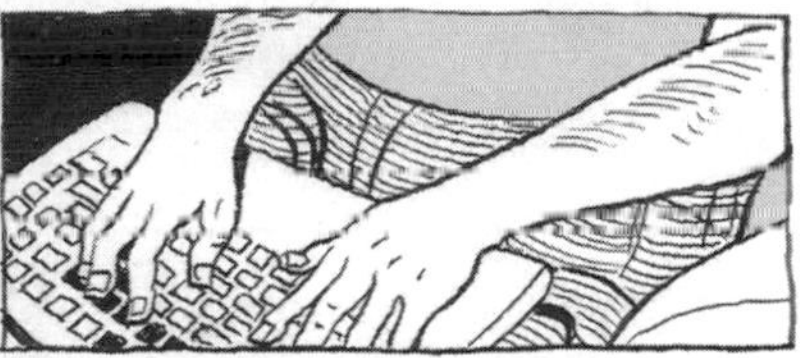

I NEED SOME PROOF THAT YOU HAVE THESE DOCUMENTS BEFORE I FLY HALFWAY ACROSS THE WORLD.

Just a very small taste, the tip of the iceberg.
(SEND)
PGP Messaging
top secret/ Comint/ Noforn
CLICK!
* NO FOREIGNERS ARE ALLOWED TO READ THE DOCUMENT
Collection directly from servers of these U.S. Service Providers: Microsoft Yahoo, Google, Facebook, Paltalk, AOL, Skype, Youtube, Apple.
THIS IS UNBELIEVABLE!
JANINE GIBSON, U.S. EDITOR OF THE GUARDIAN.
RRINNG!
JANINE, I HAVE A HUGE STORY!
I HAVE A SOURCE WHO HAS ACCESS TO WHAT SEEMS LIKE A LARGE AMOUNT OF TOP SECRET DOCUMENTS FROM THE NSA.
WHAT HE'S GIVEN ME, WHAT I JUST LOOKED AT, SHOWS SOME PRETTY SHOCKING...
HOW ARE YOU CALLING ME?
BY SKYPE. WHY?
I DON'T THINK WE SHOULD TALK ABOUT THIS ON THE PHONE...
...AND DEFINITELY NOT BY SKYPE.
YOU NEED TO COME TO NEW YORK IMMEDIATELY!

MAY 31, 2013
NEW YORK CITY
YOU NEED A NEW COMPUTER, ONE THAT HAS NEVER BEEN CONNECTED TO THE INTERNET.
AND WE NEED TO PAY CASH.
HI, JANINE.
JANINE, THIS IS LAURA POITRAS.
HI, JANINE. PLEASED TO MEET YOU.
I NEED TO SEE YOU IN MY OFFICE.
ALONE.

DEPUTY EDITOR STUART MILLER JOINED GLENN AND JANINE.
LET'S SEE WHAT YOU'VE GOT.
WOW!
HOLY SHIT!
THIS IS GOING TO SOUND CRAZY TO SOME PEOPLE.
ULTIMATELY, THE DOCUMENTS ARE WHAT MATTERS. NOT HIS IDENTITY OR HIS MOTIVES.
I SUPPOSE THIS MEANS YOU WANT TO GO TO HONG KONG TOMORROW THEN?
GIVE ME THE GO-AHEAD, AND I'LL DO IT.
LET ME THINK ABOUT IT.
SO?
THE ETERNAL QUANDARY OF REPORTERS: THE WRITER PROPOSES, THE EDITOR DISPOSES. I'VE BEEN THERE MYSELF SO MANY TIMES...

BUT HE WON'T MEET THE SOURCE UNTIL YOU AND LAURA BOTH SAY YOU'RE READY.

ON THE WAY TO THE AIRPORT.

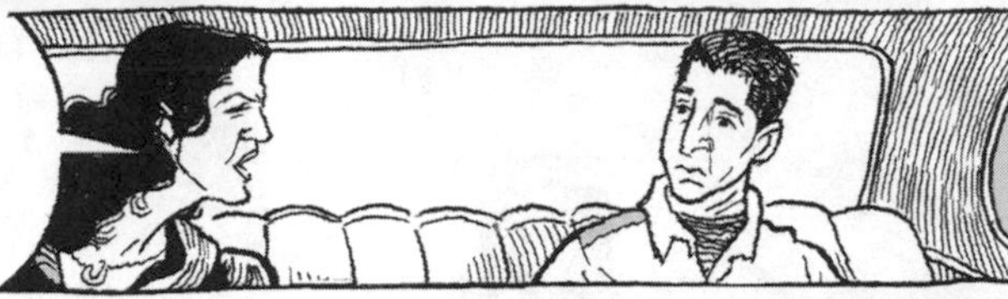

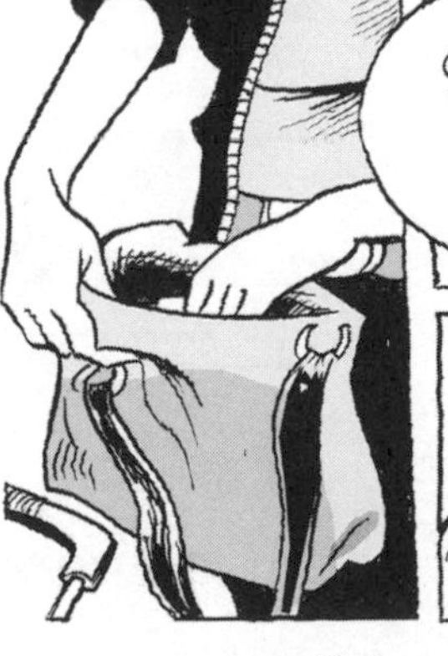

Chapter Seven

KOWLOON, HONG KONG, JUNE 3, 2013

TO THE MIRA HOTEL, PLEASE.
HOW WILL WE KNOW IT'S HIM?

WE HAVE TO GO TO THE CONFERENCE ROOMS ON THE THIRD FLOOR, AND WAIT ON A COUCH NEAR GREEN PLASTIC ALLIGATOR.

WE HAVE TWO APPOINTMENTS. ONE AT 10.00 AND ONE AT 10:20.

HE'LL BE CARRY-ING A RUBIK'S CUBE.
WE'LL ASK HIM ABOUT THE RESTAURANT AND HE'LL TELL US NOT TO GO THERE.
TAXI

WHAT'S YOUR GUESS? HOW OLD DO YOU THINK HE IS?
50? 60? PROB-ABLY NEARING RETIREMENT.

BLUE BLAZER, SHINY GOLD BUTTONS, RECEDING GRAY HAIR, SENSIBLE BLACK SHOES, A CLUB TIE.

the mira
TAXI
the mira

THE MIRA HOTEL, HONG KONG

1001-
1025
1014
GOOD, NOBODY HAS ENTERED THE ROOM.
HOW DO YOU KNOW?
THE SOY SAUCE PATTERN WOULD HAVE CHANGED ON THE NAPKIN.
DO YOU HAVE A PHONE WITH YOU?
NO.
YES, BUT IT'S BRAZILIAN. IT DOESN'T WORK HERE.
GIVE IT TO ME.
OK, NOW WE CAN TALK.
SLAM

THE DAYS OF DISCUSSION THAT FOLLOWED CULMINATED IN A SHORT VIDEO THAT WAS POSTED ON THE *GUARDIAN*'S WEBSITE. LAURA'S YEARS OF FILM WORK ON SURVEILLANCE CONTRACTORS WERE SUDDENLY ECLIPSED BY THE SIGNIFICANCE OF THIS ENCOUNTER.

the mira

ROOM 1014

MY NAME IS ED SNOWDEN, I'M 29 YEARS OLD. I WORKED FOR BOOZ ALLEN HAMILTON AS AN INFRASTRUCTURE ANALYST FOR THE NSA IN HAWAII.

WHAT ARE SOME OF THE POSITIONS THAT YOU HELD PREVIOUSLY WITHIN THE INTELLIGENCE COMMUNITY?

I'VE BEEN A SYSTEMS ENGINEER, A SYSTEMS ADMINISTRATOR FOR THE CIA, SOLUTIONS CONSULTANT, AND A TELECOMMUNICATIONS INFORMATION SYSTEM OFFICER.

K. ALEXANDER
J. CLAPPER
MR. COLE
THE NSA ROUTINELY LIES IN RESPONSE TO CONGRESSIONAL INQUIRIES ABOUT THE SCOPE OF SURVEILLANCE IN AMERICA.
IS IT POSSIBLE TO PUT SECURITY IN PLACE TO PROTECT AGAINST STATE SURVEILLANCE?
THE EXTENT OF THEIR CAPABILITIES IS HORRIFYING...
...YOU ARE NOT EVEN AWARE OF WHAT IS POSSIBLE.
WE HACK EVERYONE EVERYWHERE.
the mira
WE CAN PLANT BUGS IN MACHINES. ONCE YOU GO ON THE NETWORK I CAN IDENTIFY YOUR MACHINE. YOU WILL NEVER BE SAFE, WHATEVER PROTECTIONS YOU PUT IN PLACE...
WHAT DO YOU THINK IS GOING TO HAPPEN TO YOU?
NOTHING GOOD, BUT I COULD NOT DO THIS WITHOUT ACCEPTING THE RISK OF PRISON.

THE STUFF I SAW REALLY BEGAN TO DISTURB ME. I COULD WATCH DRONES IN REAL TIME AS THEY SURVEILLED THE PEOPLE THEY MIGHT KILL.
YOU COULD WATCH ENTIRE VILLAGES AND SEE WHAT EVERYONE WAS DOING.
IF YOUR MOTIVE HAD BEEN TO HARM THE UNITED STATES WERE THERE THINGS YOU COULD HAVE DONE?
I THINK FOR ANYONE MAKING THAT ARGUMENT, THEY NEED THINK IF THEY WERE IN MY POSITION. I LIVED A PRIVILEGED LIFE IN HAWAII, IN PARADISE, AND MADE A TON OF MONEY...
...WHAT WOULD IT TAKE TO LEAVE EVERYTHING BEHIND?
DOES YOUR FAMILY KNOW YOU ARE PLANNING THIS?
NO, MY FAMILY DOESN'T KNOW WHAT IS HAPPENING.
MY PRIMARY FEAR IS THAT THEY WILL GO AFTER MY FAMILY, MY FRIENDS, MY PARTNER, ANY-ONE I HAVE A RELATIONSHIP WITH.
IS THAT YOUR GREATEST FEAR?
mira
THE GREATEST FEAR I HAVE REGARDING THE OUTCOME OF THESE DISCLOSURES FOR AMERICA IS THAT NOTHING WILL CHANGE. THAT PEOPLE WILL SEE IN THE MEDIA ALL THESE DISCLOSURES, BUT THEY WON'T BE WILLING TO TAKE THE RISKS NECESSARY TO STAND UP AND FIGHT TO CHANGE THINGS TO FORCE THEIR REPRESENTATIVES TO ACTUALLY TAKE A STAND IN THEIR INTERESTS.

BACK AT THE *GUARDIAN*, JANINE REALIZED SHE NEEDED THE FULL BACKING OF HER STAFF AND SUPERIORS TO RUN ARTICLES BASED ON SNOWDEN'S DOCUMENTS AND TAKE ON THE WHITE HOUSE.

Hi Caitlin. I need to speak to you urgently concerning a story about U.S. surveillance activities.

I think it's best we speak by phone. Please call as soon as you can.
– Spencer

a.m.
HONG-KONG
p.m.
NEW YORK

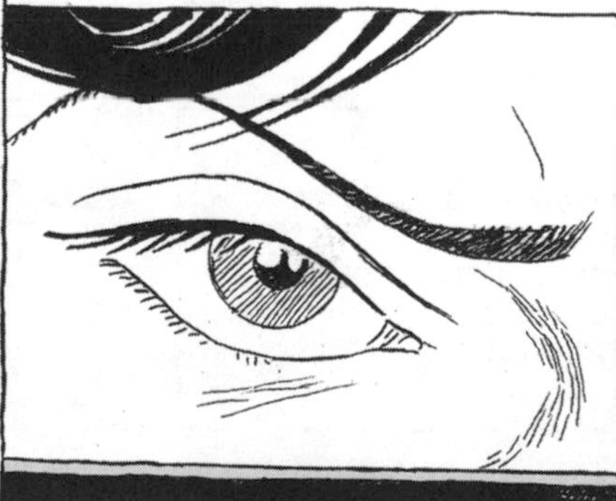

OK. BUT FROM MY PERSPECTIVE THIS HAS TO BE PUBLISHED **TODAY!** I'M NOT WILLING TO WAIT ANY LONGER!

GLENN WAS WORRIED THAT, AT THE LAST MINUTE, THE *GUARDIAN* MIGHT BUCKLE UNDER PRESSURE FROM THE WHITE HOUSE.
TICK
TICK
TICK
DO THEY HAVE ANY SORT OF DEADLINE, OR IS IT JUST WHENEVER THEY FEEL LIKE GETTING BACK TO US?
THEY SAID THEY WILL REPLY BY THE END OF THE DAY.
WHAT IF THEY DON'T RESPOND BY THEN?
WE'LL MAKE OUR DECISION THEN. ALAN IS ON A PLANE TO NEW YORK AS WE SPEAK.
ARE YOU ABLE TO PUBLISH THIS ARTICLE WITHOUT ALAN?
WE'LL SEE...
TICK
TICK
TICK
TICK
TICK
TICK
TICK
TICK

THERE WAS ANOTHER SOURCE OF PRESSURE.

DID YOU KNOW THAT THE *POST*, WHEN REPORTING THE EXISTENCE OF CIA BLACK SITES, CONCEALED THE IDENTITY OF THE COUNTRIES IN WHICH THE PRISONS WERE BASED...

...ALLOWING TORTURE TO CONTINUE?

THE *POST* IS STARTING TO ISSUE ALL SORTS OF DIRE WARNINGS.

GIVING THEM THE DOCUMENTS BOLSTERS THE VERY PREMISES WE SHOULD BE SEEKING TO SUBVERT!

I REFUSED TO GIVE ANYTHING TO THE *NEW YORK TIMES*.

THE *POST* IS NO DIFFERENT.

IT IS THE BELLY OF THE BEAST, EMBODYING ALL THE WORST ATTRIBUTES OF U.S. POLITICAL MEDIA.

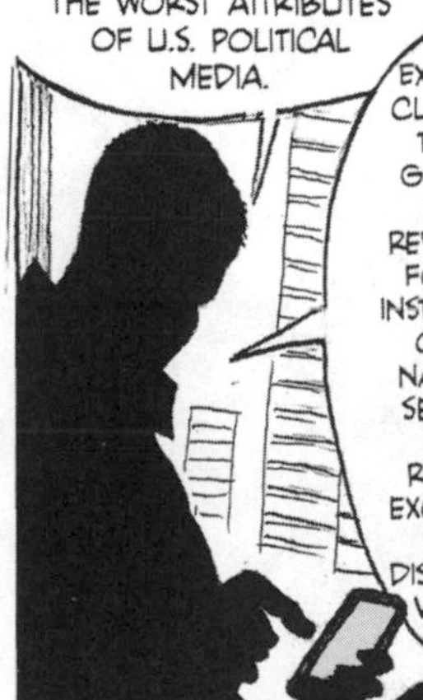

UNSURE OF HOW TO HANDLE THIS, GLENN CALLED HIS HUSBAND, DAVID MIRANDA.

GLENN, IT'S TIME FOR A DECISION. THEY NEED TO PUBLISH OR YOU NEED TO TELL THEM YOU ***QUIT!***

HONG KONG
NEW YORK
IF THEY'RE SCARED TO PUBLISH, THIS ISN'T THE PLACE FOR YOU.
YOU CAN'T OPERATE BY FEAR. THAT'S THE LESSON THAT SNOWDEN HAS TAUGHT YOU.
IF WE DON'T PUBLISH IMMEDIATELY IN THE NEXT 30 MINUTES...
...THEN I HEREBY TERMINATE MY CONTRACT WITH THE *GUARDIAN*.
SHOULD I HIT ***SEND?***
HOLD ON A SEC, SOMEONE'S TEXTING ME...
The government called back. Janine is talking to them now. - Stuart
slide to reply
NO JOURNALISTIC OUTLET WOULD PUBLISH THIS QUICKLY WITHOUT FIRST MEETING WITH US!
HOW ABOUT WE MEET SOMETIME NEXT WEEK?
YOU HAVE UNTIL 5:15 PM.
THEN WE PUBLISH.

JANINE TOLD THE WHITE HOUSE THAT THE *GUARDIAN* HAD A COPY OF A SECRET SIGNED ORDER FROM THE FOREIGN INTELLIGENCE SURVEILLANCE COURT REQUIRING TELECOM GIANT VERIZON TO HAND OVER ALL TELEPHONE CALL DATA TO THE NSA.
HONG-KONG
a.m.
NEW YORK
p.m.
RING!
THIS IS CAITLIN HAYDEN, NATIONAL SECURTITY COUNCIL SPOKESWOMAN.
HI, THIS IS CHRIS INGLIS, DEPUTY DIRECTOR OF THE NSA.
AND THIS IS BOB LITT, OFFICE OF THE DIRECTOR OF NATIONAL INTELLIGENCE.
SEAN JOYCE, DEPUTY DIRECTOR OF THE FBI.

WE HAVE A SIMPLE QUESTION. WILL YOU COMMENT ON THE COURT ORDER SIGNED BY JUDGE ROBERT VINSON OF THE FOREIGN INTELLIGENCE SURVEILLANCE COURT?
I'M SORRY. EVEN DISCUSSING A FISA COURT ORDER ON THE PHONE CONSTITUTES A FELONY.
I'LL TAKE THAT AS A *NO COMMENT* THEN?
YOU REALIZE THIS COULD JEOPARDIZE THE NATIONAL SECURITY OF THE UNITED STATES?
COULD YOU GIVE ME AN EXAMPLE OF HOW REVEALING THIS COURT ORDER COULD DO THAT?
I'M NOT IN THE HABIT OF COMMITTING FELONIES.
ALLRIGHT, WE SEEM TO HAVE REACHED AN IMPASSE.
CAN WE SPEAK TO YOUR BOSS, ALAN RUSBRIDGER?
HE'S ON A PLANE TO NEW YORK. I'M THE FINAL DECISION MAKER.
THIS IS SEAN JOYCE AT THE FBI IN WASHINGTON. CAN I SPEAK WITH DEPUTY EDITOR PAUL JOHNSON?
MARTHA, GIVE ME THE *GUARDIAN* IN LONDON.

THE COZY WORLD OF WASHINGTON, WHERE JOURNALISTS AGREED NOT TO CHALLENGE THE SECRET STATE IN EXCHANGE FOR ACCESS TO "ANONYMOUS" SOURCES, WAS ABOUT TO BE SHAKEN TO ITS FOUNDATIONS.
HELLO, THIS IS PAUL JOHNSON.
PAUL, WE'VE BEEN TALKING TO MS. GIBSON, YOUR EDITOR IN NEW YORK. WE DON'T FEEL WE'RE MAKING ANY PROGRESS.
SORRY, MATE. CAN'T HELP YOU THERE. WHILE ALAN'S IN TRANSIT, JANINE IS IN CHARGE OF THIS STORY.
NO LUCK WITH LONDON, BOB!
*@#!!
FLASH
MS. GIBSON, YOU DON'T NEED TO PUBLISH THIS. NO SERIOUS NEWS ORGANIZATION WOULD PUBLISH THIS!
I THINK YOU'LL FIND, SIR, THAT WE ARE BETTER POSITIONED THAN YOU ARE TO SAY WHAT IS A LEGITIMATE STORY.
SLAM!

Chapter Eight

CAITLIN HAYDEN AT THE WHITE HOUSE.

SPENCER ACKERMAN, AT THE *GUARDIAN*.

BY THE NEXT DAY, THE NEWS HAD GONE GLOBAL.

EXECUTIVE DIRECTOR OF THE AMERICAN CIVIL LIBERTIES UNION, ANTHONY ROMERO:

AND ON THE OBAMA ADMINISTRATION FOR NOT BEING TRUE TO ITS VALUES.

BACK IN HONG KONG, SNOWDEN WAS BOTH THRILLED AND TERRIFIED.

the mira

HONGKONG

CNN LIVE

BREAKING NEWS

LIVE GLENN GREENWALD, Columnist the Guardia

HEY!

GLENN!

IT'S EVERYWHERE! I WATCHED ALL YOUR INTERVIEWS. EVERYONE SEEMED TO GET IT!

GLENN,
THE *POST* HAS JUST PUBLISHED THEIR PRISM STORY! WE HAVE TO PUBLISH OURS NOW.

—JANINE

FIFTEEN MINUTES LATER THE GUARDIAN PUBLISHES ITS SECOND NSA STORY.
theguardian
US World Opinion Sport
NSA Prism program taps in to user data of Apple, Google and others
By Glenn Greenwald
TOP-SECRET PRISM PROGRAM CLAIMS DIRECT ACCESS TO SERVERS OF FIRMS INCLUDING GOOGLE, APPLE, AND FACEBOOK.
COMPANIES DENY ANY KNOWLEDGE OF PROGRAM IN OPERATION SINCE 2007.
AND THEN, ANOTHER BOMBSHELL:
theguardian
US edition
By Glenn Greenwald
Obama orders US to draw up overseas target list for cyber-attacks
Exclusive: Top-secret directive steps up offensive cyber-capabilities to advance US objectives around the world.
!
WHAT'S UP?
TWO NSA OFFICIALS JUST VISITED MY HOUSE IN HAWAII!
Tor
ELECTRONIC FRONTIER FOUNDATION

WITH THE MEDIA AVALANCHE SHOWING NO SIGNS OF ABATING, THE WHITE HOUSE HAD NO CHOICE BUT TO PROVIDE SOME ANSWERS.

Is it just me, or is blanket surveillance obscenely outrageous?

AN ANSWER WAS NOT LONG IN COMING:

LAURA'S VIDEO GOES VIRAL.

TWITTER LIGHTS UP RIGHT AWAY. AT FIRST, THERE ARE MANY MORE QUESTIONS THAN ANSWERS:

WHO IS EDWARD SNOWDEN?

WHERE IS HE HIDING IN HONG KONG?

WILL HE MANAGE TO ESCAPE?

"Hunting game: Edward Snowden's location unknown."

Chester Yung
@chesteryung
Wall Street Journal reporter

Posted June 10, 2013, *by Joon Ian*

"Which luxury hotel is Snowden camping out in?"

Joon Ian
@joonian
Journalist

And here's a picture of a Mira hotel room from tripadvisor.com

JUNE 10, 2013
EDWARD SNOWDEN IS NO HERO
BY JEFFREY TOOBIN, THE NEW YORKER

Some are hailing him as hero and a whistle-blower. He is neither. He is a grandiose narcissist who deserves to be in prison

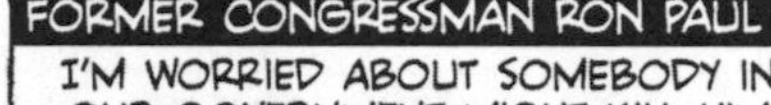

Send in some Navy Seals and shoot him in the brain. Like you think this is a game, bro? That you can embarrass the United States like this? Kill this motherfucker!

BARS
by Elpresidente

Making us look like goddamn fools. Well enough is enough. Let's just go kill his ass.

BY THE COMMON MAN FOR THE COMMON MAN

June 10, W Hotel, Hong Kong
As the media frenzy escalated, Greenwald got a call from a concerned Hong Kong fan.
RING! RING!
GLENN, YOUR LOBBY IS FILLED WITH CAMERAS AND REPORTERS. THE MEDIA IS SEARCHING FOR SNOWDEN'S HOTEL AND WILL FIND IT IMMINENTLY!
7:00
ELEMENTS
MR GREENWALD, WHERE IS EDWARD SNOWDEN?
CLICK CLICK CLICK
I'M FROM THE WALL STREET JOURNAL.
THE ASSOCIATED PRESS.
MR GREEN-WALD!
MR GREENWALD!
MR GREEN-WALD!
PSSST, I'M GILL PHILLIPS, THE GUARDIAN'S CHIEF LAWYER. IM STAYING HERE TOO.
LETS GO TO MY ROOM.
415
BUT MR. GREENWALD!
RING! RING!
Laura
WHERE'S ED?
HE GOT OUT RIGHT BEFORE THE JOURNALISTS STARTED SWARMING.

THERE WAS NOT A MOMENT TO LOSE. LIFE IMPRISONMENT OR AN EVEN WORSE FATE WAS SUDDENLY NOT JUST AN ABSTRACT THREAT. ALBERT HO, A LOCAL LAWYER, ARRANGED FOR A DISGUISED ED TO FLEE.

INSTAGRAM FROM SNOWDEN'S GIRLFRIEND, LINDSAY MILLS.

AS THOUSANDS TOOK TO THE STREETS IN SUPPORT OF SNOWDEN, THE U.S. CONGRESS WAS FORCED TO TRY TO JUSTIFY THE NATIONAL SURVEILLANCE APPARATUS.

PEOPLE AT THE NSA IN PARTICULAR HAVE HEARD A CONSTANT PUBLIC DRUMBEAT ABOUT A LAUNDRY LIST OF NEFARIOUS THINGS THEY ARE ALLEGED TO BE DOING.

BUT I WOULD RATHER BE HERE TODAY DEBATING THIS POINT THAN TRYING TO EXPLAIN HOW WE FAILED TO PREVENT ANOTHER 9/11.

THE INFORMATION GATHERED FROM THESE PROGRAMS PROVIDED THE U.S. GOVERNMENT WITH CRITICAL LEADS TO HELP PREVENT OVER 50 POTENTIAL TERRORIST EVENTS.

I WANT TO HIGHLIGHT A COUPLE. IN 2009, NSA INTERCEPTED AN EMAIL FROM A TERRORIST LOCATED IN PAKISTAN TALKING WITH AN INDIVIDUAL LOCATED INSIDE THE UNITED STATES ABOUT PERFECTING A RECIPE FOR EXPLOSIVES. THAT INDIVIDUAL WAS NAJIBULLAH ZAZI...

...WHO LATER CONFESSED TO A PLOT TO BOMB THE NEW YORK SUBWAY WITH BACKPACKS. AND NSA FOUND DAVID HEADLEY, A U.S. CITIZEN, WAS WORKING ON A PLOT TO BOMB A DANISH NEWSPAPER OFFICE THAT PUBLISHED CARTOONS OF PROPHET MUHAMMAD.

IF YOU GET A PIECE OF A NUMBER—HOW MIGHT THAT WORK INTO AN INVESTIGATION TO HELP YOU PREVENT A TERRORIST ATTACK IN THE UNITED STATES?

INVESTIGATING TERORISM IS NOT AN EXACT SCIENCE. IT'S LIKE A MOSAIC. AND WE TRY TO TAKE THESE DISPARATE PIECES AND BRING THEM TOGETHER TO FORM A PICTURE.

THERE ARE MANY DIFFERENT PIECES OF INTELLIGENCE. WE HAVE ASSETS. WE HAVE PHYSICAL SURVEILLANCE. WE HAVE ELECTRONIC SURVEILLANCE THROUGH A LEGAL PROCESS, PHONE RECORDS THROUGH AN ADDITIONAL LEGAL PROCESS.

ZAZI? HEADLEY? THE NSA HAD NOTHING TO DO WITH THEIR ARRESTS!
THOSE CLAIMS WERE DISPROVED OVER A WEEK AGO!
GOOGLE online
BuzzFeed
News Buzz Life Entertainment
June 7, 2013
Politics
Public Documents Contradict Claim Email Spying Foiled Terror Plot
Defenders of "PRISM" say it stopped subway bombings. But court documents suggest old fashioned police work nabbed Zazi.
Ben Smith
BuzzFeed Editor-in-Ch
CLICK!
June 9, 2013
theguardi
NSA surveillance played little role in foiling terror plots, experts say
Obama administration says NSA data helped make arrests in two important cases - but critics say that simply isn't true
"That's nonsense. It played no role at all in the Headley case. That's not the way it happened at all," Said an intelligence expert and former CIA operative who worked on the case and asked to remain anonymous.
CLICK!
IN YOUR ESTIMATION — JUST KIND OF GIVE US SOME INSIGHT INTO WHAT THEY'RE TALKING ABOUT. WAS THIS NSA PROGRAM SOLELY RESPONSIBLE FOR THWARTING THESE?
THERE SEEMS TO BE SOME SORT OF FUZZY MATH GOING ON HERE BECAUSE THAT'S THREE OR FOUR PLOTS, NOT DOZENS, AS WE'VE BEEN LED TO BELIEVE.
SO FAR WHAT WE HAVE HEARD TODAY ISN'T VERY MUCH DIFFERENT FROM WHAT WE HEARD LAST WEEK, AND THE AMERICAN PUBLIC WILL HAVE TO MAKE A JUDGEMENT ABOUT WHETHER THE PAYOFF, THE SMALL NUMBER OF PLOTS AVERTED HERE IN THIS COUNTRY, MAKES SENSE OF ANY POTENTIAL INFRINGEMENT TO CIVIL LIBERTIES.
CNN
ASHINGTON
PETER BERGEN, AUTHOR
The Osama I Knew
LIVE CNN
CAROL COSTELLO
NEWS
NSA SURVEILLANCE

THESE DAMN HEARINGS ARE MISSING THE POINT. IT'S NOT JUST ABOUT AN INVASION OF PRIVACY.
GOURMET BURRITOS
1920
IT'S ALSO ABOUT BLANKET SURVEILLANCE OF INNOCENT PEOPLE WHO THEN BECOME TARGETS FOR KILLING.

MATT! I SHOULD CALL MATT!

THE *GUARDIAN* HAS GOT TO CONNECT THE DOTS BETWEEN THE NSA'S SURVEILLANCE AND AN ILLEGAL WAR THAT'S CREATING MORE DANGEROUS ENEMIES.

HELLO, MAY I SPEAK WITH MATT SEATON?

I'M AFRAID HE NO LONGER WORKS HERE. MAY I HELP YOU?

I'VE GOT SOME MATERIAL I'D LIKE TO DISCUSS WITH THE *GUARDIAN*. IT'S ER...
...IT'S CONNECTED TO THE SNOWDEN FILES...

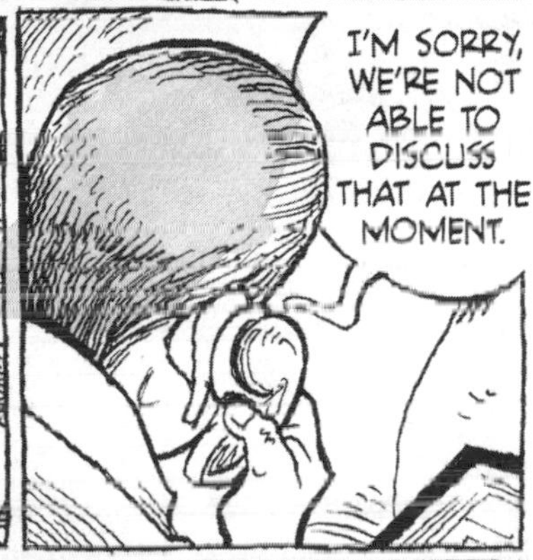
I'M SORRY, WE'RE NOT ABLE TO DISCUSS THAT AT THE MOMENT.

HMM, DO YOU THINK I COULD DROP BY BRIEFLY TO CHAT WITH YOU?

ALLRIGHT, BUT I CAN'T PROMISE YOU ANYTHING.

A FEW MINUTES LATER.
OK, I DON'T HAVE MUCH TIME. WHAT HAVE YOU GOT?
BELIEVE ME, I THINK YOU WILL FIND THIS WORTH YOUR WHILE!

GAMMA CORPORATION.
GAMM
UTIMACO.
utimaco
software
VASTECH.
VASTech Research
AND THERE'S MORE...
CONTRACTOR BROCHURES? THAT'S ALL YOU'VE GOT? HONESTLY, WE'RE MUCH TOO BUSY WITH THE SNOWDEN STUFF RIGHT NOW...
(SIGH) THESE ARE MORE THAN JUST BROCHURES. COULD YOU AT LEAST PASS THEM ON TO GLENN?
LOOK, IT'S NOTHING PERSONAL, BUT YOU'RE ON YOUR OWN, OK?
NOT EVEN THE GUARDIAN CAN BE BOTHERED ANYMORE. WHAT NOW?
NRD
I'LL JABBER POITRAS. SHE CAN REACH GREENWALD.
Hello Laura?
NO RESPONSE.
Hello? Hello?...
MAYBE JULIAN AND SARAH?
Hello, Julian? Hello, Sarah?
NOTHING THERE, EITHER.
Hello? Hello?

Chapter Nine

MEANWHILE SNOWDEN WAS BEING SHELTERED BY FILIPPINO AND SRI LANKAN REFUGEES IN HONG KONG. SARAH HARRISON OF WIKILEAKS HAD ARRIVED SECRETLY WITH ECUADOREAN SAFE PASSAGE PAPERS.
ABSOLUTELY HE'S A TRAITOR!
REPUBLICAN MICHELE BACHMANN
HE SHOULD BE PUNISHED TO THE FULLEST EXTENT OF THE THE LAW!
MIKE ROGERS, HOUSE INTELLIGENCE COMMITTEE
THEY'RE NOT GOING TO BULLY ME LIKE THEY HAVE BULLIED OTHERS...
...HOPEFULLY, WHEN I'M GONE, WHATEVER THEY DO TO ME, THERE WILL BE SOMEBODY ELSE WHO WILL DO THE SAME THING.
I REFUSE TO BE SCARED.
SARAH HARRISON, WIKILEAKS
IT WILL BE THE SORT OF INTERNET PRINCIPLE OF THE HYDRA: YOU KNOW, YOU CAN STOMP ONE PERSON, BUT THERE'S GOING TO BE SEVEN MORE OF US.
KNOCK
KNOCK
ED?
WE ARE GOING TO FILE YOUR ASYLUM REQUEST.
JONATHAN MAN, HONG KONG LAWYER

WE THINK THAT IT MIGHT TAKE SOME TIME, THOUGH.
HOW LONG?
IT'S REALLY QUITE HARD TO SAY. WE WILL DO OUR BEST, BUT...
SOME OF OUR CLIENTS HAVE BEEN WAITING FOR YEARS.
WHAT OTHER OPTIONS DO I HAVE?
ED, MY SOURCES TELL ME THAT YOU WILL PROBABLY GO TO JAIL WHILE THE COURTS HEAR YOUR CASE. IT'S REALLY NOT WORTH THE RISK.
ECUADOR IS A MUCH SAFER OPTION.
SHOULD I GO?
YOU NEED TO MAKE YOUR OWN DECISION, ED.
ECUADOR... HERE I COME!

HONG KONG AIRPORT, JUNE 23, 2013 — 10.30 AM.
CATHAY PACIFIC
FINAL BOARDING CALL FOR AEROFLOT FLIGHT SU213 FOR MOSCOW, DEPARTING AT 11:50 A.M.
D1-D2
離港
Departures
D1-D2
餐厅
Restaurants
PLEASE PROCEED IMMEDIATELY TO GATE D24!
АЭРОФЛОТ
AS WASHINGTON FRANTICALLY SCRAMBLED TO GET SNOWDEN EXTRADITED, FLIGHT SU213 TOOK OFF WITH SARAH AND ED ON BOARD, DESTINATION QUITO, ECUADOR, VIA MOSCOW.

*ENCRYPTION SOFTWARE

ECUADOREAN EMBASSY, KNIGHTSBRIDGE, LONDON. JUNE 23, 1:25PM
ASSANGE WAS NO LONGER A FREE MAN. HE HAD TAKEN ASYLUM IN ECUADOR'S EMBASSY TO ESCAPE POTENTIAL EXTRADITION TO SWEDEN.
TAP TAP TAP
Tweets
Wikileaks @wikileaks
Edward Snowden will touch down in Moscow in under one hour
wikileaks.org/wikileaks-stat
WHAT ON EARTH IS WIKILEAKS UP TO?
Edward Snowden will touch down in Moscow in under one hour
...under twenty minutes...
...ten minutes...
"I thought you were going to say "accompanied by Wikileaks fighter jets!" ;-)"
Joe Thorpe@ ...(Nothingham, UK)
If I were on the run from the US, I would choose somewhere gorgeous like the Seychelles ;-) Christine Osborne @mudskipper_ June 23 (Blue Mountain, Australia)
...three minutes...
Wow! Plot thickens again! Errol Barnett/CNN June 23 (Johannesburg, South Africa)
is Russia a democratic country? I do not get it #Snowden
Gianlucca Ugolini @GianluccaUgolini
June 23 (Rome, Italy)

THE HONG KONG AUTHORITIES TOOK ADVANTAGE OF AN ERROR IN THE U.S. DOCUMENTS TO WRIGGLE OUT OF THE CONUNDRUM.

BERKELEY, CA.

EDWARD ***"JAMES"*** SNOWDEN? HOW COME THE U.S. GOVERNMENT CAN'T GET THE NAME OF ONE OF THEIR OWN EMPLOYEES RIGHT?

MEANWHILE, IN MOSCOW:
SHEREMETYEVO AIRPORT, JULY 1-5
HAVE YOU SEEN THIS MAN?
WHERE IN THE WORLD IS EDWARD SNOWDEN?
WE KNOW THAT SOME-WHERE OUT THERE EDWARD SNOWDEN IS ON THE MOVE. HE WAS DEFINITELY IN HONG KONG.
CNN
HONG KONG
DEVELOPING STORY
TOM FOREMAN
CNN
WE HAVE WITNESSES WHO TOLD US THEY SAW HIM ON THE PLANE AND THE RUSSIANS CONFIRMED THAT HE WAS ON THIS FLIGHT.
CNN
DEVELOPING STORY
TOM FOREMAN
CNN
THE RUSSIANS NOTABLY HAVE NOT SAID HE ARRIVED IN RUSSIA. IT COULD MEAN SIMPLY THAT HE IS STILL AT THE AIRPORT, SORT OF IN A NO-MAN'S-LAND.
CNN
MOSCOW
TRANSLATION: WHETHER IN MOSCOW, QUITO, OR CARACAS, WE HAVE NO IDEA WHERE THE HELL HE IS.

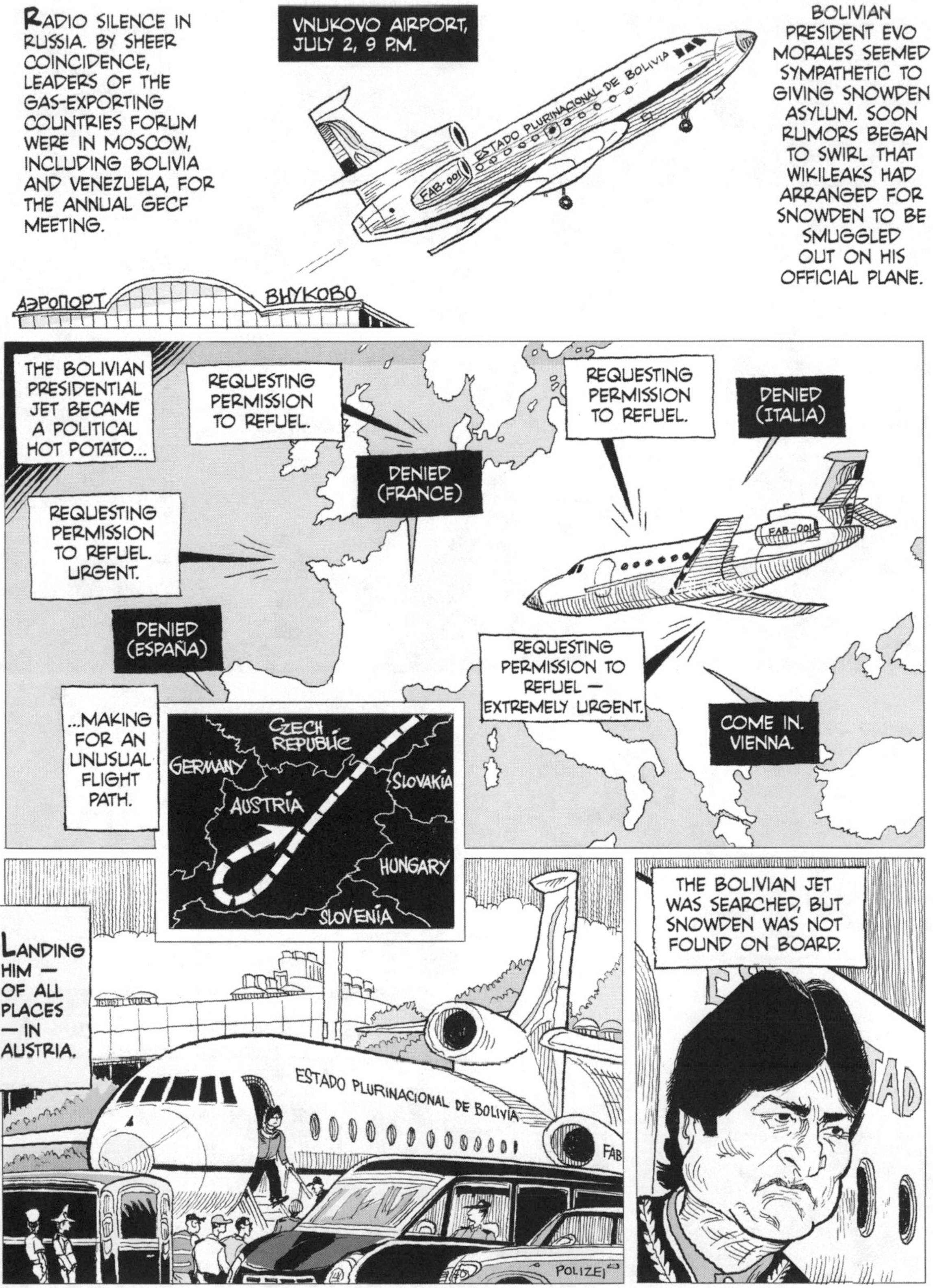

RADIO SILENCE IN RUSSIA. BY SHEER COINCIDENCE, LEADERS OF THE GAS-EXPORTING COUNTRIES FORUM WERE IN MOSCOW, INCLUDING BOLIVIA AND VENEZUELA, FOR THE ANNUAL GECF MEETING.

BOLIVIAN PRESIDENT EVO MORALES SEEMED SYMPATHETIC TO GIVING SNOWDEN ASYLUM. SOON RUMORS BEGAN TO SWIRL THAT WIKILEAKS HAD ARRANGED FOR SNOWDEN TO BE SMUGGLED OUT ON HIS OFFICIAL PLANE.

АЭРОПОРТ ВНУКОВО

THE BOLIVIAN PRESIDENTIAL JET BECAME A POLITICAL HOT POTATO...

REQUESTING PERMISSION TO REFUEL.

DENIED (FRANCE)

REQUESTING PERMISSION TO REFUEL. URGENT.

DENIED (ESPAÑA)

REQUESTING PERMISSION TO REFUEL.

DENIED (ITALIA)

FAB-001

REQUESTING PERMISSION TO REFUEL — EXTREMELY URGENT.

COME IN. VIENNA.

...MAKING FOR AN UNUSUAL FLIGHT PATH.

CZECH REPUBLIC

GERMANY

SLOVAKIA

AUSTRIA

HUNGARY

SLOVENIA

LANDING HIM — OF ALL PLACES — IN AUSTRIA.

ESTADO PLURINACIONAL DE BOLIVIA

FAB

POLIZEI

THE BOLIVIAN JET WAS SEARCHED, BUT SNOWDEN WAS NOT FOUND ON BOARD.

TAD

LEADERS ACROSS SOUTH AMERICA EXPRESSED OUTRAGE.
THEY TOLD US THE EVIDENCE WAS THERE, THAT HE *WAS* INSIDE.
JOSÉ MANUEL GARCÍA-MARGALLO, SPANISH FOREIGN MINISTER
VESTIGES OF COLONIALISM THAT WE THOUGHT WAS COMPLETELY OVERCOME!
CRISTINA FERNÁNDEZ DE KIRCHNER, PRESIDENT OF ARGENTINA
AN AFFRONT TO *ALL* AMERICA!
RAFAEL CORREA, PRESIDENT OF ECUADOR

JEN PSAKI, U.S. STATE DEPARTMENT SPOKESWOMAN:
WE HAVE BEEN IN CONTACT WITH A RANGE OF COUNTRIES THAT HAD A CHANCE OF HAVING SNOWDEN LAND OR TRAVEL THROUGH THEIR COUNTRY. BUT I AM NOT GOING TO OUTLINE WHAT THOSE COUNTRIES WERE OR WHEN THIS HAPPENED.

WHAT HAPPENED TO THE REGULAR LEGAL CHANNELS?

THIS WAS AN EXCUSE TO SCARE, INTIMIDATE, AND PUNISH ME!
COULDN'T OBAMA HAVE ASKED MOSCOW TO
EXTRADITE SNOWDEN THROUGH REGULAR CHANNELS?

SNOWDEN FINALLY RESURFACED AT SHEREMETYEVO AIRPORT, JULY 12, FOR AN INVITE-ONLY BRIEFING.
I HAD FAMILY, A HOME IN PARADISE, AND I LIVED IN GREAT COMFORT.
У меня есть семья, дом в раю, ия жил в большой комфорт
I ALSO HAD THE CAPABILITY, WITHOUT ANY WARRANT OF LAW, TO SEARCH FOR, SEIZE, AND READ YOUR COMMUNICATIONS.
У меня также была...

ANYONE'S COMMUNICATIONS AT *ANY* TIME.
THAT IS THE POWER TO CHANGE PEOPLE'S FATES!

IT IS ALSO A VIOLATION OF THE LAW: THE 4TH AND 5TH AMENDMENTS TO THE CONSTITUTION OF MY COUNTRY, ARTICLE 12 OF THE UNIVERSAL DECLARATION OF HUMAN RIGHTS, AND NUMEROUS STATUTES AND TREATIES FORBID SUCH SYSTEMS OF MASSIVE, PERVASIVE SURVEILLANCE.

I DID NOT SEEK TO ENRICH MYSELF. I DID NOT SEEK TO SELL U.S. SECRETS. I DID NOT PARTNER WITH ANY FOREIGN GOVERNMENT TO GUARANTEE MY SAFETY.
INSTEAD, I TOOK WHAT I KNEW TO THE PUBLIC. SO WHAT AFFECTS ALL OF US CAN BE DISCUSSED BY ALL OF US IN THE LIGHT OF DAY, AND I ASKED THE WORLD FOR JUSTICE.

I BELIEVE IN THE PRINCIPLE DECLARED AT NUREMBERG IN 1945: "INDIVIDUALS HAVE INTERNATIONAL DUTIES WHICH TRANSCEND THE NATIONAL OBLIGATIONS OF OBEDIENCE."
THEREFORE, INDIVIDUAL CITIZENS HAVE THE DUTY TO VIOLATE DOMESTIC LAWS TO PREVENT CRIMES AGAINST PEACE AND HUMANITY FROM OCCURRING.

INDEED, HOW ELSE CAN WE AVOID A MODERN-DAY HITLER?

Chapter Ten

FIVE MONTHS AFTER SNOWDEN FOUND REFUGE IN MOSCOW, I MET UP WITH KHALIL.
ESPRESSO ROMA
HAVE YOU BEEN KEEPING UP WITH THE SNOWDEN DISCLOSURES?
CAN'T BELIEVE ALL THE DATA THE NSA HAS BEEN COLLECTING!
97 BILLION PIECES OF DATA OVER 30 DAYS IS A STAGGERING AMOUNT BY ANY MEASURE...
...TALK ABOUT BUILDING A HAYSTACK!
WHY DO THEY COLLECT SO MUCH DATA, ANYWAY?
WELL, THE INTELLIGENCE AGENCIES HAVE ALWAYS SPIED ON ENEMIES.
BUT THIS IS MUCH MORE THAN THAT!
YES, THEY ARE COLLECTING DATA ON EVERYONE!
THE EUROPEAN UNION, THE UNITED NATIONS. SURELY THOSE ARE OUR FRIENDS?
NOT IF YOU WANT ALL THE DATA.
I HAVE TO SAY THAT THE ALPHABET SOUP AND TECHNICAL JARGON MAKE THIS HARD TO UNDERSTAND.
WHAT I DON'T GET IS HOW THEY ARE ABLE TO COLLECT ALL THIS DATA. THE SNOWDEN DOCUMENTS SHOULD COME WITH A DECODING KEY!
Espresso ROMA
LET ME TRY TO EXPLAIN HOW THE SURVEILLANCE SYSTEM WORKS.

HOW MUCH DO YOU KNOW ABOUT THE INTELLIGENCE AGENCIES?
I KNOW THE CIA, THE FBI, AND THE NSA.
THAT'S JUST THREE. THERE ARE ACTUALLY 16, NO 17 OF THEM.
WHY SO MANY?
SOME OF IT IS A BITTER TURF WAR IN WASHINGTON.
THE CIA DOES FOREIGN INTELLIGENCE WHILE THE FBI DOES DOMESTIC.
United States Intelligence Community
DEPARTMENT OF ENERGY
NSA
CIA
INR
STATE
BUREAU OF INTELLIGENCE AND RESEARCH
DEPARTMENT OF THE NAVY
AIR FORCE
OFFICE OF THE DIRECTOR OF NATIONAL INTELLIGENCE
UNITED STATES OF AMERICA
ARMY
RECONNAISSANCE
National Reconnaissance Office
COAST GUARD
DIA
DEFENSE INTELLIGENCE AGENCY
US DEPARTMENT HOMELAND SECURITY
THE PENTAGON HAS ITS OWN AGENCY, THE DIA. EVEN THE DEPARTMENT OF ENERGY HAS ONE!
DOE INTELLIGENCE
DEPARTMENT OF ENERGY
JUSTICE
NATIONAL GEOSPATIAL INTELLIGNCE
TREASURY
NATIONAL DRUG INTELLIGENCE
THERE'S ONE IN CHARGE OF RUNNING THE SATELLITE SYSTEM AND ANOTHER TRACKING DRUGS...
....AND THERE'S EVEN AN AGENCY TO OVERSEE THE OTHER SIXTEEN.

WHAT MAKES THE NSA SO IMPORTANT? WHAT DO THEY DO?
THE NATIONAL SECURITY AGENCY EVOLVED OUT OF THE NAZI CODE BREAKERS IN THE SECOND WORLD WAR.
THEY HIRE SOME OF THE CLEVEREST MATHEMATICIANS IN THE WORLD TO CONDUCT SIGNALS INTELLIGENCE.
SIGNALS INTELLI-GENCE?
IT'S ONE OF THE THREE MAJOR BRANCHES OF INTELLIGENCE. HUMAN INTELLIGENCE IS RUNNING SPIES, DOING INTERROGA-TIONS, ETC. THAT'S SOME OF WHAT THE CIA DOES.
OPEN SOURCE INTELL-IGENCE IS ANALYZING OPENLY AVAILABLE DOCUMENTS, SORT OF LIKE JOURNALISM.
SIGNALS INTELLIGENCE, BROADLY SPEAKING, IS INTERPRETING ANY SORT OF DATA SIGNALS FROM SATELLITE DATA TO OUR PHONE TRAFFIC AND EMAILS.
HOW LONG HAVE THEY BEEN LISTENING TO US?
TAPPING THE DATA FROM PHONE CALLS GOES BACK TO THE DAYS OF THE TELEGRAPH. THE ARMED FORCES SECURITY AGENCY CREATED A SYSTEM TO CAPTURE TELEGRAMS CALLED "SHAMROCK" IN THE 1940S.
IN THE 1990S THE FBI BUILT A SYSTEM CALLED CARNIVORE TO SNIFF EMAIL TRAFFIC ON COMPUTER SERVERS. THEY'VE BEEN RUMORED TO HAVE A SYSTEM CALLED MAGIC LANTERN TO HACK INTO INDIVIDUAL COMPUTERS.
BUT THE NSA HAS BUILT THE BIGGEST DATA COLLECTION SYSTEM IN THE WORLD, ENOUGH TO WATCH THE WHOLE PLANET!
THAT'S ILLEGAL, RIGHT?
IT'S UNCON-STITUTIONAL. IN FACT, THAT IS WHY SNOWDEN BLEW THE WHISTLE.

HOW MUCH CAN THEY SEE?
IMAGINE YOU COULD WANDER UNSEEN THROUGH A CITY...
...ONCE INSIDE, YOU COULD OBSERVE EVERYTHING, ANY TIME OF DAY OR NIGHT...
IMAGINE HAVING THE ABILITY TO SILENTLY RECORD EVERYBODY'S ACTIONS...
...WHETHER THEY ARE AT WORK... OR AT PLAY.

...FROM THE COMBINATIONS USED TO SECURE SAFES...
...TO THE SECRET RENDEZVOUS OF LOVERS...
...WITHOUT LEAVING A TRACE.
SUCH OMNISCIENCE COULD, OF COURSE, MAKE YOU RICH...
BUT PERHAPS WORSE, IT COULD MAKE YOU VERY POWERFUL.
GLOBALIZATION AND THE INTERNET HAVE CONNECTED ALL OUR LIVES IN A SINGLE, SEAMLESS VIRTUAL CITY...
...WHERE EVERYTHING IS ACCESSIBLE AT THE TAP OF A FINGER.
THAT SCENARIO ISN'T OUT OF SOME FUTURISTIC SCI-FI NOVEL. IT'S ALMOST REALITY RIGHT NOW.
WE STORE MONEY IN ONLINE VAULTS, CONDUCT MOST OF OUR CONVERSATIONS AND OFTEN GET FROM PLACE TO PLACE WITH THE HELP OF OUR MOBILE DEVICES.
ALMOST EVERYTHING WE DO IN THE DIGITAL REALM IS RECORDED AND LIVES ON FOREVER IN A COMPUTER MEMORY THAT, WITH THE RIGHT SOFTWARE AND THE CORRECT PASSWORDS, CAN BE ACCESSED BY OTHERS, WHETHER YOU WANT THEM TO OR NOT.

TRACKING
BUT HOW DO THEY DO IT?
I LIKE TO BREAK IT DOWN INTO FOUR METHODS: TRACKING, HACKING, MASS SURVEILLANCE, AND ANALYSIS.
LET'S START WITH TRACKING AND THE CONCEPT OF AN IMSI CATCHER.
WHAT THE HELL IS THAT?
"IMSI" STANDS FOR INTERNATIONAL MOBILE SUBSCRIBER IDENTITY. ALL MOBILE PHONES NEED ONE. IT IS THE UNIQUE NUMBER THAT ALLOWS THEM TO BE TRACKED ANYWHERE.
YOU KNOW HOW A CELL PHONE CAN WORK ANY-WHERE IN THE WORLD? THAT'S BECAUSE IT'S ALWAYS TRANSMITTING A SIGNAL TO THE NEAREST CELL TOWER AND SAYING HELLO, I'M IMSI NUMBER XYZ.
CELL PHONE
SO IF MY (HYPOTHETICAL) CELL PHONE IS ON, ANYONE WHO WORKS AT THE PHONE COMPANY KNOWS EXACTLY WHERE I AM AT ALL TIMES?
IT CAN EVEN TRACK YOU, MORE OR LESS, IF YOUR PHONE IS OFF! UNLESS YOU TAKE OUT YOUR BATTERY.
OTHER THAN THE PHONE COMPANY, WHO ELSE HAS THIS INFORMATION?
THAT'S WHERE THE IMSI CATCHER COMES IN.
A BASIC CATCHER PRETENDS TO BE A CELL PHONE TOWER AND ASKS LOCAL PHONES TO IDENTIFY THEMSELVES.

YOU MEAN, LIKE A PHONE NUMBER?
NOT QUITE. LET ME SHOW YOU...
AN INTERNAL CHIP, LIKE THIS SIM CARD, HOLDS IMSI INFORMATION SUCH AS THE PHONE NETWORK AND NUMBER
AND HOW DO THEY CATCH IT?
HMM, I NEVER TRUSTED THESE THINGS ANYWAY.
CELL TOWER
IMSI CATCHER
SO IF I HAD AN IMSI CATCHER, I COULD FOLLOW EVERYONE IN THIS AREA?
EXACTLY! FOR EXAMPLE, MANY U.S. LOCAL POLICE FORCES BUY AN IMSI CATCHER NAMED STINGRAY FROM HARRIS CORPORATION IN FLORIDA.
SO THEY CAN FOLLOW ME AROUND IF I HAVE A CELL PHONE ON ME?
YOU BETCHA!
A GOOD THING I'M PROBABLY THE LAST GUY IN BERKELEY WITHOUT ONE, THEN. LUDDITES OF THE WORLD, UNITE!

THE SECOND METHOD IS HACKING.
ANY PARENT TODAY CAN BUY SPYWARE OFF THE SHELF TO INSTALL ON THEIR KIDS' COMPUTERS.
TAKE EMAIL, FOR EXAMPLE.
AND EMPLOYERS CAN DO THE SAME TO MONITOR THEIR STAFF.
THE U.S. FOOD AND DRUG ADMINISTRATION RECENTLY BOUGHT SPYWARE FROM A COMPANY NAMED SPECTORSOFT IN FLORIDA TO SECRETLY TRACK EMAILS FROM FIVE STAFFERS THEY SUSPECTED WERE BLOWING THE WHISTLE.
WHAT THIS SOFTWARE TRIES TO DO IS TO BYPASS, GUESS, OR EVEN STEAL YOUR PASSWORD.
THAT HAPPENED TO ME! MY EMAIL PASSWORD WAS STOLEN BY CRIMINALS WHO USED IT TO TRY TO EXTORT MONEY FROM MY FRIENDS.
EXACTLY. CRIMINALS OFTEN SEND OUT EMAILS ASKING PEOPLE TO UPDATE THEIR PASSWORDS ON A FAKE SITE OR VIA SOFTWARE HIDDEN INSIDE ATTACHMENTS.
I GET THOSE ALL THE TIME!
LIKEWISE, INTELLIGENCE AGENCIES AROUND THE WORLD USE SIMILAR TRICKS TO BREAK INTO PEOPLE'S COMPUTERS AND EMAILS. IT'S A BOOMING BUSINESS.
THERE ARE ACTUAL TRADE FAIRS LIKE MILIPOL IN PARIS FOR COMPANIES LIKE GAMMA IN GERMANY AND THE APTLY NAMED HACKING TEAM IN ITALY WHO SELL SUCH TRACKING AND HACKING TECHNOLOGIES TO POLICE FORCES AND SPY AGENCIES.
NO BIZ LIKE THE SPY BIZ, HUH?

WHAT THE NSA AND THE CRIMINALS WANT TO DO IS TO TAKE CONTROL OF A PERSON'S COMPUTER WITHOUT THEIR KNOWLEDGE IN ORDER TO SPY ON THEM BY RECORDING EVERY WORD THEY TYPE, EVERY WEBSITE THEY VISIT, AND EVERY PERSON THEY CONTACT.
BOTH THE NSA AND THE CRIMINALS TRY A VARIETY OF HACKING METHODS, BEGINNING WITH "BRUTE FORCE" ATTACKS TO STEAL PASSWORDS BY TRYING MILLIONS OF PERMUTATIONS AND COMBINATIONS.
SECOND, THEY TRY TO TRICK YOU INTO REVEALING YOUR PASSWORD. ONE FAMOUS HOAX HAD THE RICHEST MAN IN THE WORLD MAKING A RATHER UNUSUAL OFFER.
I'm Bill Gates. If you click the 'share' link, I'll give you $5,000.
ONCE THEY HAVE GAINED ACCESS TO YOUR COMPUTER, THE NSA CAN TURN ON YOUR MICROPHONE OR CAMERA WITHOUT YOUR KNOWLEDGE.
CODE NAME: OPTIC NERVE
THIRD, SNOWDEN ALSO REVEALED THAT THE NSA WORKS WITH COMPUTER COMPANIES TO INSTALL SECRET BACKDOORS INTO SOFTWARE UPDATES.
SOFTWARE UPDATE:
YOUR COPY OF ADOBE ACROBAT IS OUTDATED. CLICK HERE TO UPGRADE.
CODE NAME: BULL RUN
FINALLY, THE NSA ALSO EMPLOYS BOUNTY HUNTERS TO TRAWL THE UNDERGROUND BLACK MARKET IN SOFTWARE FLAWS TO BREAK INTO COMPUTERS.

WHAT I DON'T GET IS HOW A SOFTWARE BUG IN ADOBE OR WORD CAN HELP THE NSA GET IN.
WELL, HOW DOES A VIRUS WORK IN REAL LIFE?
IT'S A BUG THAT MULTIPLIES INSIDE YOUR BODY AND ATTACKS YOUR BIOLOGICAL SYSTEMS.
BURRITOS
EXACTLY. COMPUTER VIRUSES MIMIC ACTUAL VIRUSES IN THE NATURAL WORLD.
THEY INJECT A SMALL PIECE OF COMPUTER CODE THAT CAN MULTIPLY INSIDE YOUR COMPUTER AND ATTACK IT.
TO GET IN, WHAT A VIRUS LOOKS FOR IS A **WEAKNESS** IN YOUR SYSTEM, LIKE A WOUND OR LESION IN YOUR BODY, OR A FLAW IN YOUR COMPUTER SOFTWARE.
MALWARE ATTACHMENTS AND DOWNLOADS ACT LIKE VIRAL INFECTIONS?
YES, JUST LIKE YOU CAN CATCH A COLD WHEN SOMEONE ELSE SNEEZES ON YOU. OR GET AIDS BY HAVING SEX WITH AN INFECTED PERSON.
SO THE COMPUTER "GETS SICK," IT BREAKS DOWN AND STOPS WORKING?
THAT'S ONE POSSIBILITY. BUT THE VIRUS COULD ALSO TAKE CONTROL OF YOUR SYSTEM TO PROPAGATE ITSELF. THEY CAN ALSO BE ENGINEERED TO SIPHON OFF YOUR DATA.
THAT'S WHY GOVERNMENTS AND CRIMINALS PAY BIG SUMS TO GET THEIR HANDS ON VULNERABILITIES AHEAD OF THE COMPANIES WHO MAKE THE SOFTWARE.
AN IPHONE FLAW IS WORTH ***MILLIONS,*** ESPECIALLY IF IT IS HARD TO DETECT.
YOU MEAN, THERE'S AN ACTUAL MARKET FOR THIS?
YOU BET! THERE ARE COMPANIES LIKE ENDGAME AND VUPEN THAT SPECIALIZE IN IT!

THE SNOWDEN DOCUMENTS MAKE IT SOUND LIKE THE GOVERNMENT CAN FORCE INDUSTRY INTO WORKING WITH THEM, WHETHER THEY LIKE IT OR NOT.
WELL, INDUSTRY DOES SOMETIMES OPPOSE THE GOVERNMENT.
DURING THE CLINTON ADMINISTRATION, THE NSA DESIGNED SOMETHING CALLED THE CLIPPER CHIP THAT IT WANTED INSTALLED IN ALL COMPUTERS AND TELECOMMUNICATION DEVICES.
THE GOVERNMENT CLAIMED THE CLIPPER CHIP WOULD HELP SCRAMBLE DATA TO PROTECT COMPUTER USERS FROM UNAUTHORIZED ACCESS.
WHAT THEY DIDN'T TELL ANYONE WAS THAT THE CHIP COULD ALSO TRANSMIT A SECRET SIGNAL WITH A KEY THAT THE GOVERNMENT COULD USE IF IT WANTED TO ACCESS THE SAME DATA.
SO WHAT HAPPENED?
SUSHI & ROLL
THE NSA PLAN WAS WIDELY OPPOSED ACROSS THE POLITICAL SPECTRUM. EVEN PEOPLE LIKE RUSH LIMBAUGH AND JOHN KERRY SPOKE OUT, SO THE GOVERNMENT BACKED DOWN.
BUT SNOWDEN REVEALED THAT THE NSA IS STILL UP TO ITS OLD ANTICS. THEY HAVE SITES IN TEXAS WHERE THEY CAN INTERCEPT COMPUTER PURCHASES TO INSERT EAVESDROPPING EQUIPMENT.
AND THAT'S NOT ALL. THE NSA HAS NOW GONE GLOBAL!

WHICH BRINGS US TO THE THIRD METHOD: MASS SURVEILLANCE. UNLIKE THE "ACTIVE" HACKING SYSTEMS THAT WE JUST TALKED ABOUT, IN WHICH THE NSA TARGETS SPECIFIC INDIVIDUALS, THESE "PASSIVE" TECHNOLOGIES CAN RECORD AN ENTIRE POPULATION, BY SIMPLY INTERCEPTING ALL ITS COMMUNICATIONS AND ACTIVITIES AT THE SOURCE!
HARDLY ANY SPOT ON THIS PLANET ESCAPES THIS HYDRA-LIKE NETWORK.
TYPICALLY, SUCH TECHNOLOGIES CAN ONLY BE DEPLOYED WITH THE HELP OF DATA PROVIDERS, LIKE PHONE AND INTRENET COMPANIES WHOSE DATA PIPELINE WE ALL SHARE.
THERE ARE COMPANIES LIKE COSMOS AND VASTEC THAT SELL SYSTEMS THAT CAN BE INSTALLE AT THE NATIONAL PHON EXCHANGE BY REPRE SSIVE GOVERNMENTS IN COUNTRIES LIKE EGYPT AND SYRIA.
STOP
THE COMPANIES OFFER SOPHISTICATED TOOLS LIKE "DEEP PACKET INSPECTIONS" THAT CAN TRAC EVERY DISSIDENT OR VISITOR TO A POLITICAL WEB SITE AND UNMASK EVERY PERSON WHO USES CERTAIN SOFTWARE TO ESCAPE THEIR SCRUTINY.
BUT WHAT SNOWDEN REVEALED WAS EVEN MORE STAGGERING: HE QUOTES LTNT. GENERAL KEITH ALEXANDER AS SAYING:

"WHY CAN'T WE COLLECT **ALL** THE SIGNALS **ALL** THE TIME?"
HIS GOAL HAD BECOME POSSIBLE BECAUSE MOST INTERNATIONAL DATA IS NOW TRANSMITTED VIA **FIBER OPTIC CABLE**, SO ALL YOU HAVE TO DO IS FIGURE OUT HOW TO MAKE A COPY OF THE LIGHT SIGNALS AT THE DISTRIBUTION CENTERS.

SNOWDEN REVEALED THAT THE NSA, IN COLLABORATION WITH AUSTRALIA, CANADA, NEW ZEALAND AND THE UK, * THE SO-CALLED FIVE EYES COUNTRIES, BUILT A SYSTEM CALLED TEMPORA...
* FIVE ANGLO-SAXON EYES!
USA
UK
CANADA
AUSTRALIA
NEW ZEALAND
Level (3)
Verizon
...WITH THE HELP OF SEVEN MAJOR INTERNATIONAL CABLE COMPANIES NAMELY, BT (UK), GLOBAL CROSSING (USA), INTEROUTE (UK), LEVEL 3, VIATEL (IRELAND), VERIZON BUSINESS (USA), AND VODA-FONE CABLE (UK).
TEMPORA MAKES COPIES OF THEIR DATA AT THE POINT AT WHICH THEIR UNDERSEA CABLES ENTER A COUNTRY, SUCH AS IN CORNWALL IN THE UK.
SNOWDEN'S DOCUMENTS SUGGESTED THAT THE NSA WAS ABLE TO MAKE A COPY OF A THREE-DAY BUFFER OF GLOBAL INTERNET TRAFFIC AT ANY GIVEN TIME...
...TOTALING SOME 600 MILLION "TELEPHONE EVENTS" A DAY, OR AS MUCH AS 21 PETABYTES (MILLION GIGABYTES) OF DATA.
NOW THAT'S ONE BIG HAYSTACK!

Chapter Eleven

SO, THERE'S **TRACKING, HACKING,** AND **MASS SURVEILLANCE.** THOSE ARE THREE OF THE MAIN ELEMENTS OF THE INTRICATE MAZE OF GOVERNMENT SURVEILLANCE.
BUT AS WHISTLELOWERS LIKE BILL BINNEY AND ED SNOWDEN HAVE SHOWN...
...THE NSA USES MORE ESOTERIC CODE NAMES, LIKE STELLAR WIND, PRISM, AND TEMPORA.
Shattuck
GAMES OF BERKELEY

THE IDEA WAS TO CREATE A SYSTEM BY WHICH THEY CAN SPY ON THE WHOLE WORLD AT ONCE...
...AND KEEP A RECORD OF IT FOREVER.
SNOWDEN REVEALED THAT THERE ARE TRAPDOORS...
...AND SECRET PASSAGES INTO THE STRUCTURES THAT CONNECT ALL OF US ALL THE TIME.
WITH BILLIONS OF PHONE CALLS, EMAILS, AND SKYPE VIDEO EXCHANGES EVERY DAY, HOW CAN THEY LISTEN TO ALL OF THEM?
THEY CAN'T. BUT THAT'S WHERE THE FOURTH GROUP OF TECHNOLOGY COMES IN.
ANALYSIS?

THE NSA HAS LOCK-SMITHS ON CALL TO HELP CREATE MASTER EYS FOR ALL THE ROOMS.
WITH THE HELP OF BOUNTY HUNTERS, THEY CAN STALK US...
...AND BUILD PROFILES OF OUR LIVES AND SECRETS TO USE AGAINST US.
WANTED
YES. WHAT THEY WANT IS NOT SO MUCH WHAT YOU SAY BUT THE METADATA—WHO YOU TALK TO AND WHEN.
THEY'RE LOOKING FOR PATTERNS?
EXACTLY! THEY CLAIM THAT IF THEY CAN MAP ALL OUR SOCIAL NETWORKS, THEY WILL BE ABLE TO STOP POTENTIAL TERRORIST PLOTS BEFORE THEY HAPPEN.

GOVERNMENTS EVERYWHERE PRIZE METADATA.
Leverage Metadata!
YaHoo! MAIL
in box
Drafts
Sent
Trash
content
contacts
Can analyze this automatically
Login
Password
Subject
Text
Sender
Receiver
Contact
List
QOSMOS
Analyze Commun
YaHoo! MAIL
contacts
Contact List
QOSMOS
HERE'S ANOTHER ONE THAT JULIAN OBTAINED FROM A U.S. COMPANY NAMED GLIMMERGLASS.
Select Optional Signals to Access
International Gateway
Submarine Cable Landing Station
Point of Presence (POP/Central Office
Mobile and Fixed Line, data, Voice and video, social media
SMS
NOW TAKE A LOOK AT WHAT THEY CLAIM THEY CAN DO WITH THE DATA.
Monitor Internet, Webmail, VoIP, Mobile
Facebook chart
TOP SECRET

IN 2011 WIKILEAKS GAVE ME A STASH OF BROCHURES FROM SPY COMPANIES.
THIS ONE IS FROM QOSMOS.
ons Patterns
Login
Password
Email address
Content
Login
Pword
Email
Content
Login
Pword
Email
Content
Login
Pword
Email
Content
QOSMOS
Increasing Number of Targets and Communications: Use Metadata to manage the huge amounts.
1. Entire traffic of an intercepted ISP
2. Relevant metadata only
Metadata feeds
Metadata can even replace content
Major storage savings
nications
·Acquire
·Select
·Distribute
Copyright 2011
Glimmerglass Networks Confidential
Select remotely
Glimmerglass Networks
THOSE ARE THE UNDERWATER FIBER-OPTIC CABLE STATIONS THAT SNOWDEN TALKED ABOUT!
AT INDUSTRY DEMOS THAT I ATTENDED IN PARIS AND DENVER, THE COMPANIES BOASTED THAT THEIR SOFTWARE COULD CREATE PROFILES OF SPECIFIC INDIVIDUALS FROM THEIR PHONE, EMAIL, AND SOCIAL MEDIA DATA.
WHO WERE THEY SELLING THIS TECHNOLOGY TO?
ANY GOVERNMENT THAT COULD PAY— FROM ASSAD'S REGIME IN SYRIA TO MUBARAK'S IN EGYPT AND GADDAFI'S IN LIBYA.
THE USUAL SUSPECTS.

BUT IT'S NOT JUST REPRESSIVE REGIMES WHO WANT THIS TECHNOLOGY.
LET ME GUESS. OBAMA IS ALSO A MAJOR PLAYER IN THIS BUSINESS.
THAT'S RIGHT. THE REST OF THE WORLD GOT A GLIMPSE OF THIS WHEN SNOWDEN REVEALED **X-KEYSCORE.**
X-WHAT?
X-KEYSCORE.
HERE, TAKE A LOOK.
Plug-ins Extract and Index Metadata Into Tables
Sessions
Session
(Processing engine)
(Database)
User queries
Phone numbers
email addresses
Log ins
User activity
Metadata tables
Full log
THE NSA BOASTED THAT IT COULD ANSWER QUESTIONS LIKE: "MY TARGET SPEAKS GERMAN BUT IS IN PAKISTAN.
HOW CAN I FIND HIM?"
AND "MY TARGET USES GOOGLE MAPS TO SCOPE TARGET LOCATIONS, CAN I USE THIS INFORMATION TO DETERMINE HIS EMAIL ADDRESS?"
HOW DO THEY ANSWER SUCH QUESTIONS?
IT'S CALLED "GRAPH ANALYSIS."

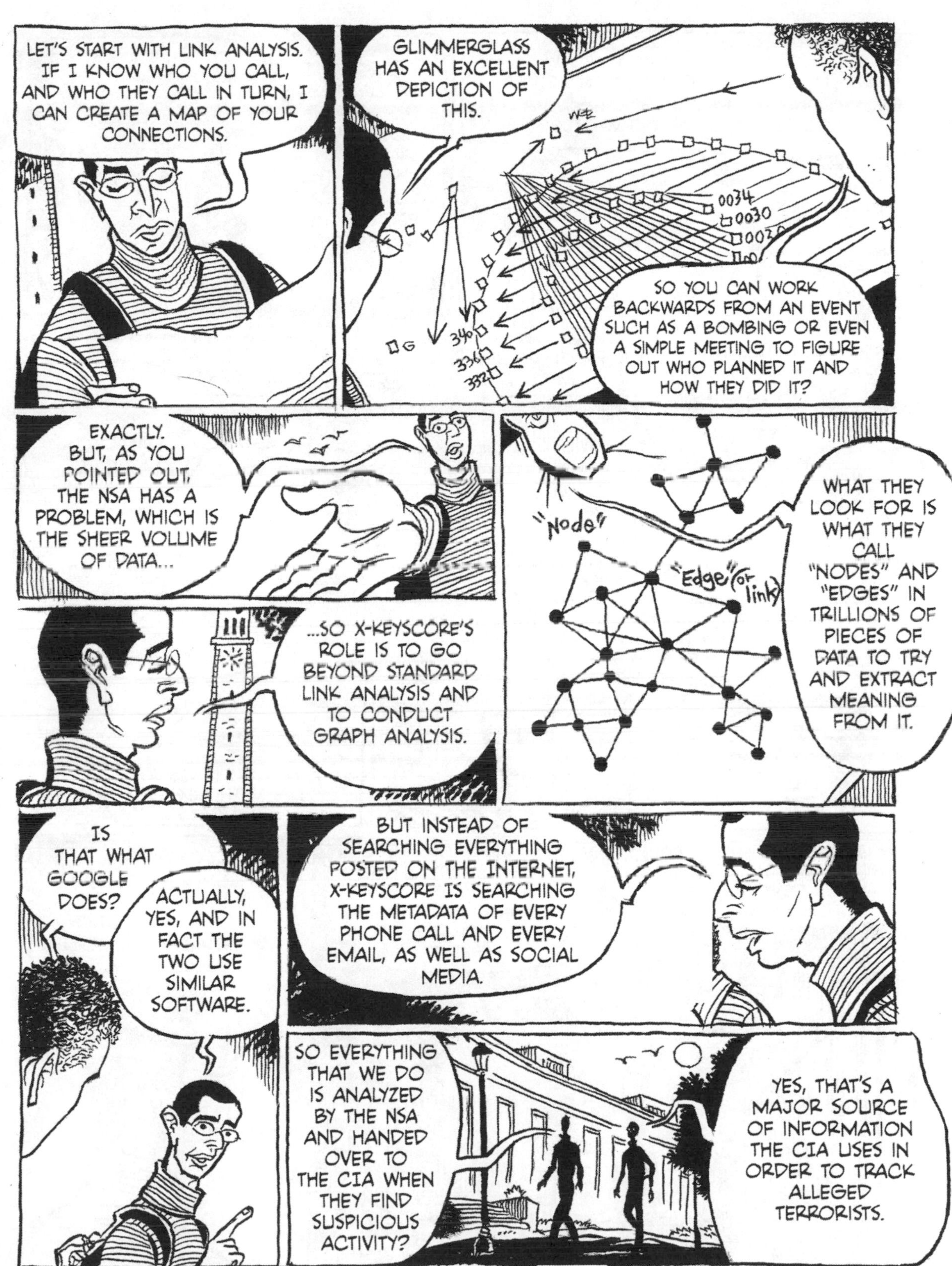

LET'S START WITH LINK ANALYSIS. IF I KNOW WHO YOU CALL, AND WHO THEY CALL IN TURN, I CAN CREATE A MAP OF YOUR CONNECTIONS.
GLIMMERGLASS HAS AN EXCELLENT DEPICTION OF THIS.
SO YOU CAN WORK BACKWARDS FROM AN EVENT SUCH AS A BOMBING OR EVEN A SIMPLE MEETING TO FIGURE OUT WHO PLANNED IT AND HOW THEY DID IT?
EXACTLY. BUT, AS YOU POINTED OUT, THE NSA HAS A PROBLEM, WHICH IS THE SHEER VOLUME OF DATA...
"Node"
"Edge" (or link)
WHAT THEY LOOK FOR IS WHAT THEY CALL "NODES" AND "EDGES" IN TRILLIONS OF PIECES OF DATA TO TRY AND EXTRACT MEANING FROM IT.
...SO X-KEYSCORE'S ROLE IS TO GO BEYOND STANDARD LINK ANALYSIS AND TO CONDUCT GRAPH ANALYSIS.
IS THAT WHAT GOOGLE DOES?
ACTUALLY, YES, AND IN FACT THE TWO USE SIMILAR SOFTWARE.
BUT INSTEAD OF SEARCHING EVERYTHING POSTED ON THE INTERNET, X-KEYSCORE IS SEARCHING THE METADATA OF EVERY PHONE CALL AND EVERY EMAIL, AS WELL AS SOCIAL MEDIA.
SO EVERYTHING THAT WE DO IS ANALYZED BY THE NSA AND HANDED OVER TO THE CIA WHEN THEY FIND SUSPICIOUS ACTIVITY?
YES, THAT'S A MAJOR SOURCE OF INFORMATION THE CIA USES IN ORDER TO TRACK ALLEGED TERRORISTS.

IN FACT, SNOWDEN SAYS THAT IT WAS WHEN HE STUMBLED UPON THE CONNECTION BETWEEN THE NSA AND THE DRONE PROGRAM, THAT HE DECIDED TO BLOW THE WHISTLE.
THE STUFF I SAW REALLY BEGAN TO DISTURB ME. I COULD WATCH DRONES IN REAL TIME AS THEY SURVEILLED THE PEOPLE THEY MIGHT KILL.
MICHAEL HAYDEN, THE FORMER HEAD OF BOTH THE NSA AND THE CIA, EVEN ADMITTED PUBLICLY THAT THIS WAS TRUE.
PANEL DISCUSSION MAY 11, 2014.
JOHNS HOPKINS UNIVERSITY
WE KILL PEOPLE BASED ON METADATA.
0:20/4 h
DURING THE IRAQ WAR, GENERAL RICHARD CODY CREATED A U.S. ARMY DRONE BATTALION NAMED ODIN, WHICH HE ARMED WITH DATA SENSORS TO HUNT FOR PEOPLE PLANTING BOMBS TO BLOW UP AMERICAN TANKS.
ODIN? YOU MEAN THE ONE-EYED NORSE GOD OF WAR AND DEATH?
YES, THE MILITARY LOVES TO USE MYTHOLOGICAL SYMBOLS.
IN COUNTRIES LIKE PAKISTAN AND YEMEN, THE CIA USES AN NSA DEVICE CALLED GILGAMESH.
THE SEMI-DIVINE KING WHO RULED OVER ANCIENT MESOPOTAMIA?
YEP! THIS GILGAMESH IS A DEVICE ATTACHED TO THE BOTTOM OF A DRONE TO TRACK CELL PHONES AND CAPTURE THEIR METADATA.
ACCORDING TO SNOWDEN, ONE NSA UNIT ADOPTED AN UNOFFICIAL MOTTO: ***WE TRACK 'EM, YOU WHACK 'EM.***

Chapter Twelve

IN APRIL 2015, OBAMA HIMSELF REVEALED PROOF THAT THE FLAWED USE OF SUREVILLANCE DATA IN DRONE WARFARE WAS KILLING INNOCENT PEOPLE.
NBC NEWS WASHINGTON
...BOTCHED DRONE STRIKE IN PAKISTAN!
THIS MORNING, I WANT TO EXPRESS OUR GRIEF AND CONDOLENCES TO THE FAMILIES OF TWO HOSTAGES.
ONE AMERICAN, DR. WARREN WEINSTEIN, AND AN ITALIAN, GIOVANNI LO PORTO, WERE TRAGICALLY KILLED IN A U.S. COUNTER-TERRORISM OPERATION.
GIOVANNI LO PORTO
WARREN WEINSTEIN
BASED ON THE INTELLIGENCE THAT WE HAD OBTAINED AT THE TIME, INCLUDING HUNDREDS OF HOURS OF SURVEILLANCE...
...WE BELIEVED THAT THIS WAS AN AL QAEDA COMPOUND, AND THAT NO CIVILIANS WERE PRESENT.
IN A NATIONAL PUBLIC RADIO INTERVIEW, DAVID ROHDE, A FORMER TALIBAN HOSTAGE, SPOKE OUT ABOUT LO PORTO AND WEINSTEIN'S DEATHS.
THE HEAT SENSORS ONLY SHOWED FOUR MILITANTS. THE CIA OPERATORS WERE STUNNED TO SEE THEM PULL OUT *SIX* BODIES!

AND DIDN'T REPRIEVE PUBLISH A REPORT LAST YEAR ON HOW THE U.S. CLAIMS TO HAVE KILLED THE SAME PERSON MULTIPLE TIMES?

AMY GOODMAN
DEMOCRACY NOW!

JOINING US FROM BERLIN IS JENNIFER GIBSON, A STAFF ATTORNEY AT REPRIEVE, AUTHOR OF THE NEW REPORT "YOU NEVER DIE TWICE."

THIS SHOWS THAT THE ACCIDENTAL KILLING OF WEINSTEIN AND LO PORTO WAS BY NO MEANS AN ABERRATION!

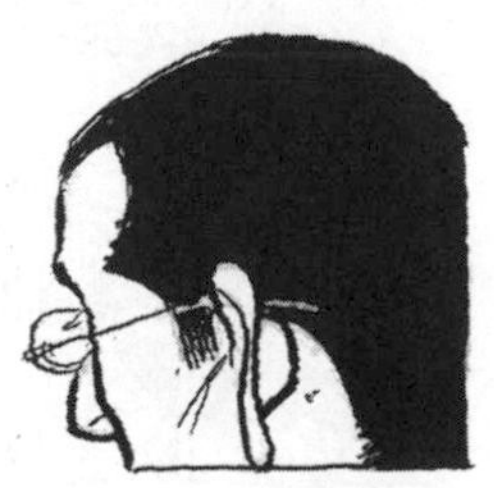

SO I SAT DOWN AND FISHED OUT ALL THE HUMAN RIGHTS REPORTS THAT I HAD COLLECTED OVER THE YEARS TO SEE IF I COULD SPOT ANY OTHER PATTERNS.

AMNESTY ALSO RELEASED A VIDEO ABOUT THE DEATH OF 68-YEAR-OLD MAMANA BIBI ONE AFTERNOON IN OCTOBER 2012.

OR TAKE YEMEN. WE HAVE THREE REPORTS: ONE BY AL KARAMA, A SWISS NGO, ONE BY HUMAN RIGHTS WATCH, AND ANOTHER BY THE OPEN SOCIETY FOUNDATION IN NEW YORK.

AL KARAMA HAS RELEASED VIDEOS OF DRONE STRIKES ON WEDDING CONVOYS.
AL KARAMA

THIS WAS A CONVOY FOR A WEDDING WITH MORE THAN 70 PEOPLE.
0:06
THIS WAS THE BRIDE'S CARRIAGE.

THIS IS THE HUMAN RIGHTS WATCH REPORT.
HUMAN RIGHTS WATCH
ONE OF THE MEN THEY INTERVIEWED WAS FAISAL BIN ALI JABER, WHOSE BROTHER-IN-LAW AND NEPHEW WERE KILLED IN A DRONE STRIKE IN 2012.

FINALLY, THE OPEN SOCIETY REPORT:
ALI SALEH AL-QAWELI KILLED JANUARY 23, 2013
WE HAD HOPED THAT AMERICA WOULD COME TO THE REGION WITH EDUCATIONAL AND DEVELOPMENT PROJECTS AND SERVICES, BUT IT CAME INSTEAD WITH AIRCRAFTS TO KILL OUR CHILDREN.

THESE REPORTS CONTRADICT STATEMENTS BY SENATOR FEINSTEIN AND THE CIA, WHO INSIST THAT THE NUMBER OF INNOCENT VICTIMS OF DRONE STRIKES IS LESS THAN 10.
ONE HAS TO ASK WHAT IT WOULD TAKE FOR THE OBAMA ADMINISTRATION TO BE INVESTIGATED FOR WHAT APPEAR TO BE WAR CRIMES. THEY EVEN REFUSED TO MEET WITH UN EXPERTS LOOKING INTO DRONE DEATHS IN PAKISTAN.

IN THIS VIDEO, WE SEE A PAKISTANI WOMAN WORKING WITH TWO EXPERTS IN FRONT OF A COMPUTER TO MAP OUT A DRONE STRIKE THAT TOOK PLACE ON OCTOBER 4, 2010.
LAWYER
WITNESS
MODEL MAKER

MY FAMILY AND I WERE HAVING BREAKFAST.
AND THEN IT HAPPENED: WE HEARD A VERY LOUD BANG. THE HOUSE SHOOK AND A LOT OF EARTH FELL FROM THE CEILING.
FIVE PEOPLE WERE KILLED IN THIS DRONE ATTACK.
05:46
HD::vimeo

AND HERE'S A VIDEO OF BEN EMERSON, THE UN SPECIAL RAPPORTEUR ON HUMAN RIGHTS, TALKING TO AL JAZEERA ABOUT WHAT THEY CONCLUDED.

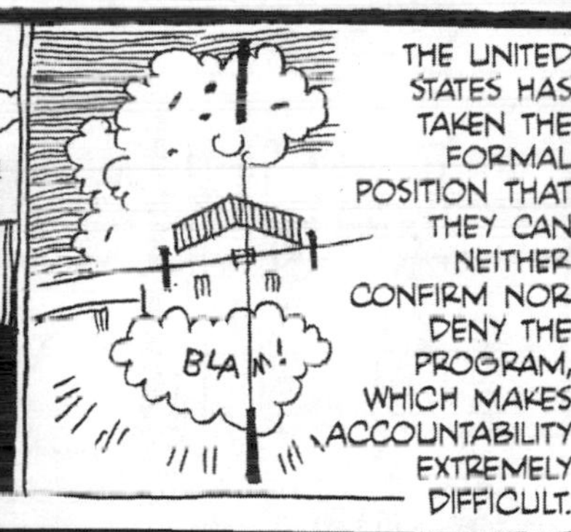
THE DIFFICULTY OVER THE LAST 5 YEARS HAS BEEN THE COMPLETE FAILURE OF A PROPER FACTUAL INVESTIGATION ON THE GROUND AS TO WHAT IS REALLY HAPPENING.
THE UNITED STATES HAS TAKEN THE FORMAL POSITION THAT THEY CAN NEITHER CONFIRM NOR DENY THE PROGRAM, WHICH MAKES ACCOUNTABILITY EXTREMELY DIFFICULT.
BLAM!

IN THE COURSE OF YOUR INVESTIGATION, HAVE YOU SEEN ANY EVIDENCE THAT WOULD SUGGEST THAT WAR CRIMES HAVE TAKEN PLACE AS A RESULT OF THESE DRONE STRIKES?
I CANNOT SAY THAT I HAVE COME ACROSS EVIDENCE THAT WAR CRIMES HAVE BEEN COMMITTED.
4:22 /5:42

BUT SURELY THE EVIDENCE OF ALL THESE FIRSTHAND WITNESSES, FAMILY MEMBERS, AND INTERNATIONAL NGOS THAT HUNDREDS OF INNOCENT PEOPLE HAVE BEEN KILLED MUST BE WORTH SOMETHING?

WHAT I THINK THESE REPORTS SHOW IS WHAT I'VE ALWAYS SUSPECTED. THE DRONES ARE USING FAULTY DATA.
HUMAN RIGHTS WATCH REPORT
UNITED NATIONS
REPRIEVE
STANFORD UNIVERSITY REPORT
COLUMBIA UNIVERSITY
KARAMA RISING FOR DIGNITY
IF THEY CAN LISTEN TO OUR CALLS, READ OUR EMAILS, AND WATCH US FROM ABOVE,
SURELY THEY KNOW EVERYTHING ABOUT US?
SNOWDEN ONCE SAID THAT THE PROBLEM WAS NOT THAT WE DIDN'T HAVE ENOUGH DATA.
THE PROBLEM WITH MASS SURVEILLANCE IS THAT WE'RE PILING MORE HAY ON A HAYSTACK.
BUT MORE HAY WON'T HELP YOU FIND A NEEDLE!
LIKEWISE, MORE BAD DATA CAN JUST MAKE YOU MORE LIKELY TO MAKE MISTAKES.
STATISTICIANS OFTEN CALL THIS "CONFIRMATION BIAS," THAT IS, THE TENDENCY TO INTERPRET NEW EVIDENCE AS CONFIRMATION OF ONE'S EXISTING BELIEFS.
WHAT INFORMATION ARE THEY LOOKING FOR?
WEAPONS FOR ONE. MEN WHO BUY GUNS, TRAVEL WITH GUNS, FIRE GUNS.
BUT JUST LIKE IN TEXAS, PEOPLE IN YEMEN OWN LOTS OF GUNS. THAT DOESN'T MAKE THEM ALL TERRORISTS.

MAYBE THAT'S WHY THEY OFTEN BOMB WEDDINGS. IN THE MIDDLE EAST, PEOPLE OFTEN FIRE SHOTS INTO THE AIR TO CELEBRATE, LIKE WE USE FIREWORKS.
EXACTLY!
DRONES USE THERMAL IMAGERY TO DETECT GUNS AND PEOPLE.
IT WOULD BE EASY...
...FOR A DRONE OPERATOR TO CONFUSE ONE MAN WITH A GUN FOR ANOTHER MAN WITH A GUN.
HOW COMMON IS THIS?
IN APRIL 2011, A DRONE OPERATOR SHOT AND KILLED TWO MARINES...
...IN FULL BATTLE UNIFORM IN BROAD DAYLIGHT IN AFGHANISTAN, BECAUSE THEY FIRED WEAPONS.
DOES ANYONE KEEP TRACK OF THESE KILLINGS?
WELL, THE UNITED STATES RARELY PUBLISHES DATA ON DRONE STRIKES BUT I HAVE SOME STATISTICS HERE...
...FROM MY FORMER EMPLOYER, THE BUREAU OF INVESTIGATIVE JOURNALISM.
OUT OF 646 PROBABLE DRONE STRIKES IN PAKISTAN, SOMALIA, AND YEMEN, SOME 22 PERCENT OF PEOPLE KILLED WERE INNOCENT CIVILIANS, INCLUDING 225 CHILDREN.

IF 22 PERCENT OF PEOPLE KILLED BY DRONES ARE INNOCENT, THE DRONE OPERATORS MUST BE USING SOME PRETTY BAD DATA.
IS THERE A WAY TO TAKE A LOOK AT THIS DATA?
NO, NOT REALLY. ALTHOUGH I DO HAVE SOME DOCUMENTS FROM ONE STRIKE.
HOW DID YOU GET A HOLD OF THEM?
THE ACLU USED THE FREEDOM OF INFORMATION ACT TO GET A COPY OF A MILITARY INVESTIGATION INTO CIVILIAN DEATHS.
HOW DETAILED ARE THESE DOCUMENTS AND WHAT DO THEY SHOW?
WELL, OVER 2,000 PAGES WERE RELEASED. MOST OF THEM CONSIST OF INTERVIEWS WITH THE SOLDIERS WHO TOOK PART IN THE STRIKE.
IT IS QUITE CLEAR THAT THERE WAS A DISPUTE OVER WHAT THEY COULD SEE.
THE PILOT THOUGHT SOME VILLAGERS WERE ABOUT TO KILL U.S. SOLDIERS. IN THE HEAT OF THE MOMENT, THE CREW DECIDED NOT TO TAKE A CHANCE, DESPITE THE POOR QUALITY OF THE VIDEO FEED.
BUT AT LEAST ONE SOLDIER TRIED TO WARN THE OTHERS?
YES, THERE'S A TRANSCRIPT OF EVERYTHING THE SOLDIERS SAID...
...DURING THE STRIKE.
IN REAL TIME?
TAKE A LOOK AT THE TRANSCRIPT FOR YOURSELF.

Chapter Thirteen

WHAT THIS SHOWS IS THAT THE TSUNAMI OF DATA MAKES IT ALL TOO EASY TO JUMP TO THE WRONG CONCLUSIONS.
A TEAM OF U.S. SOLDIERS WERE SEARCHING FOR INSURGENTS IN URUZGAN PROVINCE, AT THE CRACK OF DAWN.
THE MILITARY PROVIDED BACK-UP FROM THE AIR WITH A PREDATOR DRONE, A WARTHOG GUN-SHIP, AND TWO KIOWA HELICOPTERS.
A DRONE CREW IN NEVADA SPOTTED THREE VEHICLES HEADING TOWARD THE SOLDIERS AND AS-SUMED THAT THEY WERE ON THEIR WAY TO KILL THE AMERICANS.
THAT'S A LOT OF EYES ON THE GROUND!
AND YET THEY WERE HAVING A HARD TIME MAKING SENSE OF WHAT WAS HAPPENING, SOME OF THE OBSERVERS BEING HALF A WORLD AWAY.
SO THERE WERE TWO GUYS IN NEVADA, RIGHT?
YES, THE DRONE PILOT AND THE CAMERA OPERATOR. THEY ALSO HAD A COMMANDER WITH THEM.
IS IT THE JOB OF THE CAMERA OPERATOR TO LOOK FOR THE TARGETS?
TO A CERTAIN EXTENT. THE PEOPLE WHO REALLY STUDY THE IMAGES BEING BEAMED BACK BY SATELLITE ARE THE VIDEO ANALYSTS IN FLORIDA.
AND THERE ARE ALSO PILOTS WATCHING FROM THE WARTHOGS IN AFGHANISTAN?
YES. IN FACT, THOSE KIND OF COMBAT AIR PATROLS HAVE AS MANY AS 186 PEOPLE INVOLVED AT ANY GIVEN TIME.
I CAN SEE HOW THAT COULD BREED A LOT OF CONFUSION!
A CLASSIC CASE OF TOO MANY COOKS.

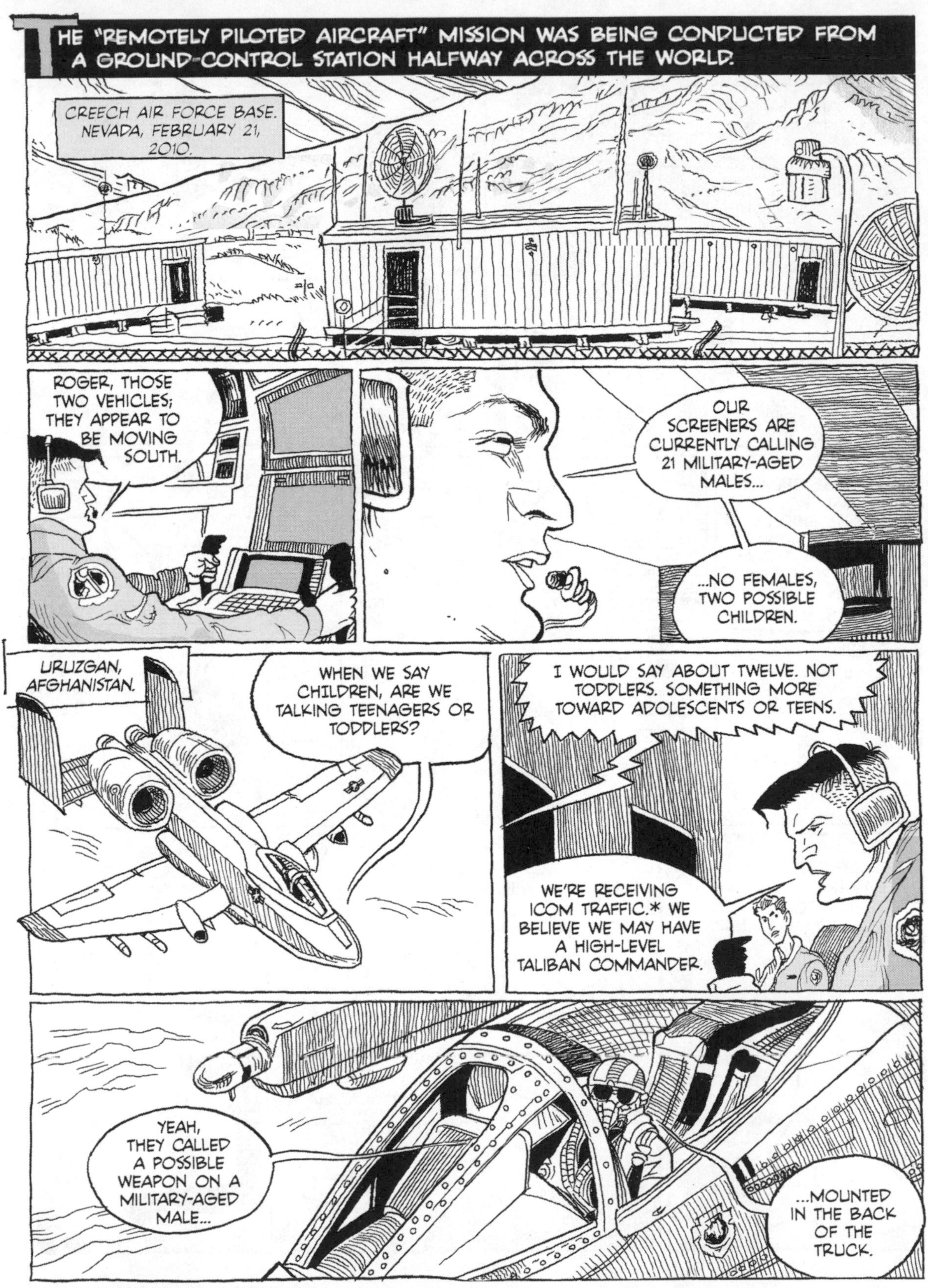

* VOICE CHATS INTERCEPTED BY SURVEILLANCE.

SCREENER SAID AT LEAST ONE CHILD NEAR SUV.
BULLSHIT! WHERE?
I DON'T THINK THEY HAVE KIDS OUT AT THIS HOUR.
I KNOW THEY'RE SHADY, BUT COME ON!
STAND BY ON THAT ZOOM OUT AND METADATA.
A SWEET #@!# TARGET, GEEZ!
LEAD VEHICLE ON THE RUN AND BRING THE HELOS IN!
BLAM!
TAKE A LOOK AT THIS ONE! IT WAS HIT PRETTY GOOD. IT'S A LITTLE TOASTY!
WOW!
THAT TRUCK IS SO DEAD!

THE THING IS, NOBODY RAN!
YEAH, THAT WAS WEIRD.
UH, HAVE YOU BEEN ABLE TO POSITIVELY IDENTIFY ANY INDIVIDUALS WITH WEAPONS AT THIS POINT?
MISSION COORDINATOR, FLORIDA.
TASK FORCE SOUTH IS COMING IN, UH, TO CONDUCT A SEARCH...
...TAKE PICTURES OR WHAT-NOT.
RATATATATATATATATATATATAT
YEAH, THERE'S DEFINITELY NO WEAPONS ON THE GUYS IN THE MIDDLE VEHICLE.
LET'S KEEP LOOKING AT...WHATEVER!
WE LOOKED AT ALL OF THEM AND I DON'T THINK THAT ANY OF THEM HAVE WEAPONS!

THEY'RE TRYING TO SURRENDER, I THINK.

I PERSONALLY WOULDN'T BE COMFORTABLE SHOOTING AT THESE PEOPLE.

I BELIEVE POSSIBLY TWO OF THESE, MAYBE THREE, WERE FEMALE. THEY WORE BRIGHT-COLORED CLOTHING.

HE'S CALLING FEMALES? THEY SAID **21 MALES,** NOT FEMALES!

DUDE, WE WATCHED THESE GUYS STOP MULTIPLE TIMES, AND EVERY TIME THEY WERE ALL WEARING ALL BLACK AND ONLY *AFTERWARD* DID WE EVER SEE ANY COLOR!

IT'S POSSIBLE THE... THE WOMEN AND CHILDREN NEVER GOT OUT OF THE CAR AT THE STOPS...

BE ADVISED WE DO HAVE WHAT LOOKS TO BE THREE WOMEN AND TWO CHILDREN POSSIBLY TRYING TO SURRENDER...

THREE HOURS LATER, THE MILITARY FINALLY DISPATCHED A RESCUE TEAM.
RATATATATATATATATATATAT
UNITED STATES OF AME
AFGHAN OFFICIALS CONDEMN DEADLY NATO AIR STRIKE.
PBS NEWSHOUR
SUNDAY'S AIRSTRIKE TARGETED THREE VEHICLES. TWENTY-SEVEN WERE KILLED...
...INCLUDING FOUR WOMEN AND A CHILD.
SHUKRA BARAKZAI, MEMBER OF THE AFGHAN PARLIAMENT.
IT'S VERY DIFFICULT FOR US, FOR THE PEOPLE OF AFGHANISTAN...
...TO FIND ANSWERS WHY CIVILIANS ARE DYING. WE DON'T HAVE ANY ANSWER FOR THIS.
LIEUTENANT GENERAL RICK PARKER, INTERNATIONAL FORCE IN AFGHANISTAN
IF WE KILL THE PEOPLE THAT WE'RE TRYING TO PROTECT, OUR CREDIBILITY IS UNDERMINED.

GENERAL STANLEY MCCHRYSTAL, TOP U.S. COMMANDER IN AFGHANISTAN, MEETS WITH PRESIDENT HAMID KARZAI.
WE WANT TO APOLOGIZE...
...TO THE AFGHAN PEOPLE.
I PLEDGE TO STRENGTHEN OUR EFFORTS TO REGAIN YOUR TRUST.
TO BUILD A BETTER AFGHANISTAN.
ISAF
WE PROMISE TO UNDERTAKE A THOROUGH INVESTIGATION.
TO PREVENT THIS FROM HAPPENING AGAIN.
ISAF
MAJOR GENERAL JAMES O. POSS, AIR FORCE INVESTIGATOR
THREE MONTHS LATER...
WE KNOW FROM OUR INVESTIGATION OF THE STRIKE THAT TECHNOLOGY CAN SOMETIMES GIVE YOU A FALSE SENSE OF SECURITY...
...THAT YOU CAN SEE EVERYTHING, THAT YOU CAN HEAR EVERYTHING...
...THAT YOU *KNOW* EVERYTHING.

THE INVESTIGATION EVENTUALLY CONCLUDED THAT THE THREE VEHICLES THEY WERE TRACKING WERE JUST VILLAGERS ON THEIR WAY TO THE MARKET.
READING THIS, IT IS PAINFULLY CLEAR THAT THE IMAGERY ANALYSTS SUSPECTED THERE WERE CHILDREN IN THE CONVOY FROM THE VERY START.
YES, THE ANALYSTS DID MAKE THE CORRECT CALL.
IF ONLY THE PILOTS AND THE COMMANDERS HAD LISTENED TO THEM.
THE OBAMA ADMINISTRATION SEEMS TO THINK THAT "COLLATERAL DAMAGE" IS ACCEPTABLE UNLESS AMERICANS OR EUROPEANS GET KILLED.
IF ONLY THE ANALYSTS WOULD SPEAK OUT.
MAYBE THEY'D BE WILLING TO TALK TO YOU OFF THE RECORD?
HMMM...
...I GUESS IT'S WORTH A TRY.

Chapter Fourteen

I STARTED TO OBSESSIVELY RESEARCH EVERYTHING I COULD ABOUT DRONE PILOTS. I STUMBLED ON TWO FILMS THAT HAD USED MY FOOTAGE FROM THE JIRGA IN PAKISTAN.

I WONDERED IF BRANDON WOULD BE ABLE TO HELP ANSWER MY QUESTIONS ABOUT SURVEILLANCE AND THE DRONE WAR. PERHAPS ROBERT GREENWALD WOULD INTRODUCE ME TO HIM.

TONJE SCHEI HAD ALSO INTERVIEWED BRANDON FOR HER OWN FILM. I WONDERED IF SHE COULD HELP ME TRACK HIM DOWN?

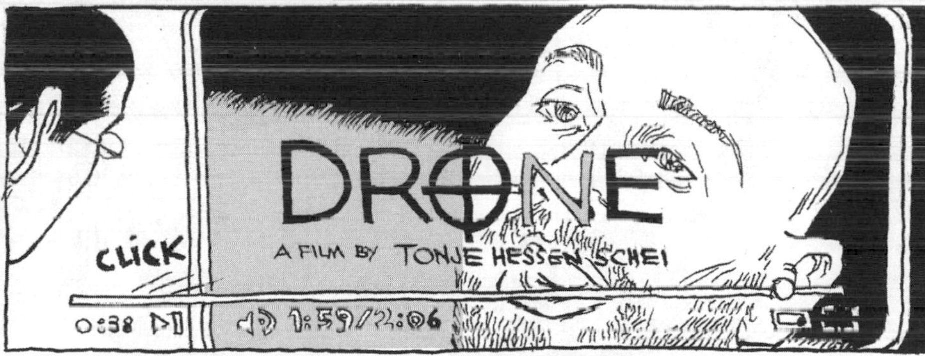

HOW ODD: WHY WOULD THIS GUY SUFFER FROM PTSD IF HE WAS BASED HERE IN THE STATES...

A FEW WEEKS LATER...
HELLO BRANDON, THANK YOU FOR AGREEING TO TALK TO ME.
I'M SORRY I'VE BEEN SO HARD TO REACH. I'VE BEEN IN REHAB.
I WAS TOLD THAT YOU HAVE PTSD. HOW DID THAT HAPPEN?
THE DRONE PROGRAM. I'LL GIVE YOU AN EXAMPLE: I WATCHED A MAN BLEED TO DEATH. A MISSILE WE FIRED TOOK OFF ONE OF HIS LEGS RIGHT ABOVE THE KNEE.
IT WAS HORRIFYING TO KNOW HOW EASY IT WAS TO KILL SOMEONE.
I FELT LIKE A COWARD BECAUSE I WAS HALFWAY ACROSS THE WORLD AND THE GUY NEVER EVEN KNEW I WAS THERE.
WHERE WERE YOU?
IN A TRAILER AT THE NELLIS AIR FORCE BASE IN NEVADA.
WHAT WAS YOUR JOB?
I WAS AN AIR FORCE SENSOR OPERATOR, WHICH MEANS I OPERATED THE DRONE CAMERAS. BUT I COULD ALSO FIRE MISSILES, LIKE THE PILOTS WHO SAT NEXT TO ME IN NEVADA.
EVERYONE ELSE THINKS THAT WE ARE VIDEO GAME WARRIORS...
...THAT WE'RE A JOKE.

BUT IT'S MORE THAN JUST A NINTENDO GAME, ISN'T IT?
IT IS. THE DRONE WAR IS VERY COMPLEX.
THE WHOLE OPERATION PROCEDURE IS LIKE A WEB; YOU'RE DEALING WITH PEOPLE FROM MULTIPLE LOCATIONS FROM ALL OVER THE WORLD.
HOW DO YOU COORDINATE WITH THEM?
THERE'S A CHAT PROGRAM. THAT'S THE EASIEST WAY TO COMMUNICATE, BECAUSE OF THE SATELLITE DELAY.
HOW OFTEN DID YOU TAKE PART IN STRIKES?
I WAS 20 WHEN I JOINED. I TOOK MY FIRST SHOT A FEW WEEKS AFTER MY 21ST BIRTHDAY.
ONE TIME, THIS FIGURE RUNS AROUND THE CORNER, TOWARD THE FRONT OF THE BUILDING.
I ASKED THE PILOT, "DID THAT LOOK LIKE A CHILD TO YOU?"
AFTER I FINISHED WORK THAT DAY, I CALLED MY MOM AND I TOLD HER I KILLED PEOPLE, AND I DON'T FEEL GOOD ABOUT IT.
AND SHE'S LIKE, "GOOD, THAT'S HOW IT SHOULD FEEL. YOU SHOULD NEVER NOT FEEL THAT WAY."
THE PILOT SAID, "PER THE REVIEW, IT'S A DOG."
WHEN I QUIT SIX YEARS LATER, THEY GAVE ME A CERTIFICATE FOR 1,626 KILLS.
HOW DID THAT MAKE YOU FEEL?
THE NUMBER MADE ME SICK TO MY STOMACH. THIS ISN'T A VIDEO GAME.
COMBAT IS COMBAT. KILLING IS KILLING.

I WAS SOON ABLE TO TRACK DOWN SEVERAL OTHER DRONE PERSONNEL. MOST OF THEM WERE ALSO SUFFERING FROM PTSD.

POLITICIANS SPEAK ABOUT DRONES BEING PRECISION WEAPONS THAT MAKE SURGICAL STRIKES. BUT TO ME, IT'S COMPLETELY RIDICULOUS TO MAKE THESE STATEMENTS. THEY ARE AS FLAWED AS THEY CAN BE WITH PEOPLE OPERATING THEM FROM ACROSS THE WORLD.
HOW DID THAT AFFECT YOU?
I WAS SHAKING. YOU SEE SOMEONE DIE BECAUSE YOU SAID IT WAS OK TO KILL THEM.
I MAY NOT HAVE BEEN ON THE GROUND IN AFGHANISTAN, BUT I WATCHED PARTS OF THE CONFLICT IN GREAT DETAIL ON A SCREEN FOR DAYS ON END. I KNOW THE FEELING YOU EXPERIENCE WHEN YOU SEE SOMEONE DIE.
I SOON REALIZED THAT THIS IS *REAL*. IT'S SO PRIMITIVE, RAW, STRIPPED-DOWN DEATH. IT'S NOT A JOKE.
DID YOU EVER GET USED TO IT?
NEVER! SOMETIMES I WOULD JUST GO TO THE BATHROOM AND JUST SIT ON THE TOILET, JUST SIT THERE AND CRY.
WHEN YOU ARE EXPOSED TO IT OVER AND OVER AGAIN, IT BECOMES LIKE A SMALL VIDEO, EMBEDDED IN YOUR HEAD, FOREVER ON REPEAT.
MY PSYCHOLOGIST CALLED MY FIRST SERGEANT AND SAID I WAS HIGH RISK FOR SUICIDE. HE RECOMMENDED THAT I BE MOVED TO ANYTHING THAT WASN'T WATCHING PEOPLE DIE.
WHAT WOULD YOU SAY TO THE PEOPLE WHO SAY THAT THIS IS AN EFFECTIVE PROGRAM?
I'D START WITH: HOW MANY WOMEN AND CHILDREN HAVE YOU SEEN INCINERATED BY A HELLFIRE MISSILE? AND HOW MANY MEN HAVE YOU SEEN CRAWL ACROSS A FIELD, TRYING TO MAKE IT TO THE NEAREST COMPOUND FOR HELP WHILE BLEEDING OUT FROM SEVERED LEGS?

ALTHOUGH BRANDON AND HEATHER WERE HELPFUL, I KNEW I NEEDED MORE DETAILS ABOUT FLAWS IN THE TARGETING TECHNOLOGY.
CIAN WEST-MORELAND.
HI, CIAN. THANKS FOR TALKING TO ME ABOUT DRONES. WHAT WAS YOUR ROLE IN THE PROGRAM?
I WAS AN AIR FORCE RADIO TECHNICIAN. I HELPED BUILD THE COMMUNICATIONS INFRASTRUCTURE FOR THE U.S. MILITARY'S DRONE PROGRAM IN AFGHANISTAN.
AND YOU HAVE PTSD FROM THESE STRIKES?
YES, I HAVE NIGHTMARES OF A CHILD NEXT TO AN ASH-COVERED BODY AND LOOKING AT ME, AS IF I HAD DONE IT.
WERE YOU DIRECTLY INVOLVED IN DRONE STRIKES?
TECHNICALLY, NO. MY JOB WAS TO PERFORM DIAGNOSTICS ON ALL OF THE EQUIPMENT.
SO WHY THE TRAUMA?
WELL, THE RESPONSIBILITY FOR KILLING THE PERSON IS DIVIDED. SO NOBODY FEELS THE FULL RESPONSIBILITY. YOU HAD IMAGERY ANALYSTS, THE COMMANDER, AND THE PILOTS.
BUT I BELIEVE THAT *ALL* PARTIES INVOLVED ARE RESPONSIBLE FOR EVERYTHING THE DRONE PROGRAM DOES. TO SAY OTHERWISE WOULD MEAN THAT NOBODY IS RESPONSIBLE, AND THAT THE ACT OF KILLING IS DEVOID OF MORALITY.
THIS IS NOT A WORLD I AM WILLING TO LIVE IN. I REFUSE TO AVERT MY ATTENTION FROM MY ROLE IN THIS MACHINE OF DEATH AND RUINED LIVES.
IF THERE WAS ANY WAY I COULD STOP THIS WAR AND APOLOGIZE FOR WHAT I HAVE DONE, I WOULD.

I KNOW WE CAN'T CHANGE THE PAST, CIAN, BUT DO YOU THINK YOU COULD BE WILLING TO HELP ME UNCOVER THE TRUTH ABOUT THE DRONE PROGRAM?
WHAT DO YOU WANT TO KNOW?
COULD YOU HELP ME UNDERSTAND THE FLAWS IN THIS TECHNOLOGY, ESPECIALLY SINCE YOU WORKED ON THE TECHNICAL ASPECTS?
MOST OF IT ISN'T SECRET, YOU KNOW? THERE'S A LOT OF PUBLIC INFORMATION ON IT, IF YOU KNOW WHERE TO LOOK.
OH YEAH? LIKE WHAT?
LIKE ON THE DISTRIBUTED COMMON GROUND SYSTEM. THAT SYSTEM IS ALWAYS BREAKING DOWN.
DCGS? REALLY? I SAW A DEMO OF IT AT A DIA CONFERENCE IN DENVER A COUPLE OF YEARS AGO.
START THERE AND SEE WHAT YOU CAN FIND. I HAVE A FRIEND, LISA, WHO WORKED ON IT. SHE CAN HELP EXPLAIN IT TO YOU.
WOW! THIS COULD BE THE CONNECTION TO THE SNOWDEN REVELATIONS THAT I HAVE BEEN LOOKING FOR. WAS THE NSA SENDING YOU SURVEILLANCE DATA?
TO BE HONEST, WHEN YOU'RE IN THE DRONE PROGRAM, YOU'RE ISOLATED. OPERATORS, ANALYSTS, LEADERS ALL WORK SEPARATELY. ALL YOU HEAR IS VOICES TELLING YOU WHAT TO DO.
YOU'RE EXPOSED TO JUST A LIMITED AMOUNT OF THE SPECTRUM.
STILL, THIS IS A GOOD LEAD, THANK YOU!

A HIGH-LEVEL MILITARY VIDEO BRIEFING SOON CONFIRMED THAT PTSD WAS VERY COMMON.
LAST JUNE, I VISITED CREECH AIR FORCE BASE AND SAW OUR REMOTELY PILOTED AIRCRAFT MISSION FIRSTHAND. TALKS WITH THE PILOTS AND THE SENSOR OPERATORS SUGGESTED TO ME THAT THIS IS A FORCE THAT IS UNDER SIGNIFICANT STRESS.
I LEARNED THAT MANY OF OUR EXPERIENCED OPERATORS ARE NEARING THE END OF THEIR ACTIVE-DUTY SERVICE COMMITMENT, WHICH MEANS THEY WILL LEAVE THE AIR FORCE.
2:21
RIIIING!
MATT
MATT SEATON HERE, PRATAP, I'M AT THE *NEW YORK TIMES* NOW. I JUST SAW A STORY ABOUT DRONE PILOTS. ARE YOU STILL WORKING ON THE SUBJECT?
I AM. IN FACT, I'VE BEEN INTERVIEWING AIR FORCE VETERANS WITH PTSD. THAT'S ONE OF THE REASONS THEY ARE QUITTING.
PTSD? AREN'T THEY JUST SITTING IN NEVADA USING JOYSTICKS?
THAT'S THE WEIRD THING, MATT. JUST BECAUSE THEY ARE ON THE OTHER SIDE OF THE WORLD DOESN'T MEAN THAT THEY DON'T EXPERIENCE WAR UP CLOSE.
IN FACT, THE JUNIOR IMAGERY ANALYSTS SAY THAT THEY HAVE THE SAME PSYCHOLOGICAL SYMPTOMS AS GROUND TROOPS.
AND NOW THEY WANT TO SPEAK OUT AGAINST THE WAR BASED ON THEIR PERSONAL EXPERIENCES.
HMM... THAT MIGHT MAKE A GOOD OPINION PIECE. WANT TO SEND ME A SHORT PROPOSAL?
FOR THE ***NEW YORK TIMES?***

AFTER A NUMBER OF REVISIONS, MATT SENT MY PIECE TO HIS COLLEAGUES.
PRATAP, WE GOT A GOOD, POSITIVE RESPONSE FROM THE READERS.
WHEN YOU SAY "READERS," YOU MEAN THE *NEW YORK TIMES* OPINION EDITORIAL TEAM?
YES, THE REVOLUTIONARY COMMITTEE THAT DECIDES WHETHER AN OP-ED GOES INTO PRINT OR TO THE GUILLOTINE!
KHALIL, GUESS WHAT? THE *NEW YORK TIMES* IS GOING TO PUBLISH AN OP-ED BY ME ON THE DRONE PILOTS!
WOW, CONGRATS! YOU'RE GOING TO BE MORE FAMOUS THAN ELVIS!
FAMOUS, SHMAMOUS! BUT THIS COULD CONVINCE OTHER DRONE PERSONNEL TO STEP FORWARD TO TALK TO ME NOW.
MY ARTICLE FINALLY APPEARED IN PRINT ON JULY 14, 2015.
Our Drone War Burnout
JULY 14, 2015
By PRATAP CHATTERJEE
...We need far greater transparency about the targeted killing operations. For a full accounting of the impact of America's drone wars, at home and abroad, our representatives in Congress must hear directly from the veterans.

THE REACTION TO MY OP-ED WAS INSTANT AND POSITIVE. MANY PEOPLE WANTED TO SUPPORT MY WORK.
RACHEL OLDROYD, EDITOR-IN-CHIEF, BUREAU OF INVESTIGATIVE JOURNALISM
PRATAP, I'D LIKE YOU TO TALK TO CROFTON ON OUR DRONE TEAM. PERHAPS WE CAN WORK TOGETHER?
TAKE THAT, IAIN!
RACHEL WAS PROMOTED AFTER MY FORMER BOSS, IAIN OVERTON, RESIGNED. SHE'S BEEN MUCH MORE RECEPTIVE TO MY WORK.
CROFTON BLACK, BUREAU OF INVESTIGATIVE JOURNALISM
WE'VE CREATED A DATABASE OF KEY DRONE CONTRACTS. I'D BE HAPPY TO HELP DIG UP DATA FOR YOU IF YOU THINK IT COULD HELP.
THAT COULD BE JUST WHAT I NEED!
CORI CRIDER OF REPRIEVE
HI, PRATAP, REPRIEVE HAS SUED THE GOVERNMENT OVER DRONE KILLINGS ON BEHALF OF VICTIMS, AS YOU MAY KNOW. DO YOU THINK THAT THE WHISTLEBLOWERS YOU'VE TALKED TO MIGHT BE WILLING TO HELP US?
HMM, TOUGH CALL.
I REALLY WASN'T SURE HOW THE WHISTLEBLOWERS WOULD REACT. BUT THE IDEA OF PUTTING FORMER SOLDIERS IN TOUCH WITH THE VICTIMS INTRIGUED ME.
YOU KNOW, THE CONCEPT OF TRUTH AND RECONCILIATION BETWEEN OPPOSING PARTIES CAN HELP BOTH SIDES HEAL. ADVOCATES OF THIS APPROACH CALL THIS RESTORATIVE JUSTICE.
REP
LISA MAGARRELL, NATIONAL SECURITY AND HUMAN RIGHTS CAMPAIGN, THE OPEN SOCIETY FOUNDATION, NEW YORK.
WE ARE WORKING WITH A NUMBER OF HUMAN RIGHTS GROUPS TO TACKLE THE ISSUE OF DRONES. WOULD YOU BE AVAILABLE TO BRIEF THEM AT A MEETING THIS NOVEMBER?
COULD BE VALUABLE ALLIES.
GIVEN THAT NOBODY IN CONGRESS HAD RESPONDED TO MY CALL FOR PUBLIC HEARINGS, THIS BRIEFING SEEMED LIKE THE NEXT BEST OPTION.

Chapter Fifteen

BY SHEER COINCIDENCE, THE OPEN SOCIETY GATHERING COINCIDED WITH TONJE SCHEI'S FILM RELEASE IN NEW YORK, SO BRANDON WAS IN TOWN TO MEET WITH REPORTERS.
CORI, I'VE CONVINCED BRANDON BRYANT AND TONJE SCHEI TO COME GIVE A BRIEF TALK AT THE OPEN SOCIETY. THERE ARE SEVERAL OTHER WHISTLEBLOWERS WHO WOULD BE WILLING TO MEET WITH US.
ABSOLUTELY. I THINK IT WOULD BE VERY EDUCATIONAL FOR US TO HEAR ABOUT THE PERSPECTIVE OF THE SOLDIERS WHO SEE THESE KILLINGS FIRSTHAND.
GREAT, I'LL ASK TONJE IF SHE CAN HELP US SET UP A TIME.
A FEW DAYS LATER, AT THE BRIEFING.
CORI, TONJE, BRANDON.
WOULD ANY OF THE DRONE PERSONNEL CONSIDER MEETING VICTIMS' FAMILIES?
I'VE HAD THE CHANCE TO MEET WITH MANY VICTIMS' FAMILIES IN PAKISTAN MYSELF. I THINK YOU WILL FIND THEIR PERSONAL STORIES TO BE VERY POWERFUL. PERHAPS IT MIGHT EVEN HELP YOU WITH YOUR PTSD?
I WOULD BE HAPPY TO DISCUSS IT WITH THE OTHERS.
WE HAVE A YEMENI CLIENT BY THE NAME OF FAISAL.
HE HAS BEEN SEEKING ANSWERS FOR THE DEATH OF HIS NEPHEW AND THAT OF HIS BROTHER-IN-LAW. HE'D APPRECIATE ANY HELP.

TONJE ARRANGED FOR CORI AND ME TO MEET THE WHISTLEBLOWERS FOR DINNER.

OK, BRANDON AND CIAN HAVE CONVINCED THE OTHERS TO SEE YOU.

TWO NEW WHISTLEBLOWERS — MICHAEL AND STEPHEN. BOTH WORKED AS SENSOR OPERATORS.

BUT THEY ARE STILL STRUGGLING WITH PTSD, JUST SO YOU KNOW.

I UNDERSTAND HOW HARD THIS MUST BE FOR THEM AND I PROMISE THAT WE ARE JUST HERE TO LISTEN TO WHATEVER THEY HAVE TO SAY. THAT IN ITSELF IS VERY VALUABLE TO ME.

CORI AND I HOPPED IN A TAXI AND HEADED OVER TO JOIN THE GROUP AT A RESTAURANT.

PRATAP, BEFORE YOU TALK TO ANYONE, I'D LIKE YOU TO MEET THEIR LAWYER.

SURE, I'M HAPPY TO RESPECT ANY GROUND RULES THEY MAY HAVE.

THIS IS JESSELYN RADACK FROM WHISTLEBLOWER AND SOURCE PROTECTION PROGRAM AT EXPOSE FACTS.

HER CLIENTS ARE INTRIGUED BY THE IDEA OF MEETING VICTIMS' FAMILIES BUT DON'T WANT TO GET IN TROUBLE.

HI JESSELYN, I'M AWARE THAT YOUR CLIENTS HAVE TO BE CAREFUL ABOUT WHO THEY MEET. WHY DON'T WE JUST LIMIT THE TALK TO THE ACCURACY OF THE PROGRAM?

MICHAEL AND STEPHEN WERE HAPPY TO TALK ABOUT THE FAILURES OF THE PROGRAM.

I'M STEPHEN LEWIS FROM TEXAS.

I'M MICHAEL HAAS. I LIVE IN ELKO, NEVADA. I USED TO TRAIN NEW RECRUITS.

WHAT DO YOU GUYS THINK OF THE DRONE WAR?

LET'S JUST SAY THIS. IT WASN'T VERY ACCURATE. IT'S BEEN VERY TRAUMATIC FOR ME SO I REALLY DON'T WANT TO DISCUSS IT.

WHAT ABOUT YOU, MICHAEL?

I WAS PRETTY FUCKED UP WHEN I WAS DEPLOYED. I DID BATH SALTS. THERE WAS A LOT OF COKE... ...EVERYONE DRANK.

WE USED TO CALL ALCOHOL "DRONE FUEL" BECAUSE IT KEPT THE PROGRAM GOING. IT WAS EVERYWHERE.

YOU START TO DO THESE PSYCHOLOGICAL GYMNASTICS TO MAKE IT EASIER TO DO WHAT YOU HAVE TO DO — "THEY DESERVED IT," "THEY CHOSE THEIR SIDE."

YOU HAD TO KILL PART OF YOUR CONSCIENCE TO KEEP DOING YOUR JOB EVERY DAY AND IGNORE THOSE VOICES TELLING YOU THIS WASN'T RIGHT.

THEY SAID THEY WOULD CONSIDER REPRIEVE'S REQUEST TO MEET WITH VICTIMS' FAMILIES BUT PTSD KICKED IN AGAIN, AND THEY DROPPED OUT OF SIGHT, APART FROM CIAN.

PRATAP, I'VE FOUND SOMEONE WHO WOULD BE WILLING TO MEET FAISAL. LISA LING USED TO BE A DCGS OPERATOR AND HAS ALREADY BEEN TO AFGHANISTAN TO MEET VICTIMS' FAMILIES.

IT TURNED OUT THAT LISA LIVED JUST THIRTY MINUTES AWAY FROM ME.

I KNEW I NEEDED TO GAIN HER TRUST FIRST.

FIRST RULE: I'M NOT A LEAKER!

THAT'S REASONABLE. I'M JUST HERE TO HEAR YOUR STORY.

I SERVED IN THE MILITARY FOR OVER TWENTY YEARS. I RETIRED IN 2012.

I WORKED ON THE DRONE PROGRAM AS A TECHNICAL SERGEANT. WHEN I DISCOVERED HOW INACCURATE IT WAS, I KNEW I HAD TO MAKE AMENDS FOR THE MISTAKES THAT I HAD MADE.

CIAN TOLD ME THAT YOU'VE BEEN TRYING TO TRACK DOWN VICTIMS' FAMILIES IN AFGHANISTAN?

YES, I WENT TO MEET THE VICTIMS OF THE 2010 URUZGAN STRIKE.

THEN I THINK YOU'D BE INTERESTED IN MEETING FAISAL, WHOSE FAMILY WAS ALSO TARGETED BY MISTAKE. HUMAN RIGHTS WATCH WROTE A REPORT ABOUT THE INCIDENT.

LISA WAS FULLY ON BOARD. NOW I NEEDED A WAY TO SET UP THE MEETING WITH FAISAL. AS LUCK WOULD HAVE IT, LAURA POITRAS CAME TO MY AID.
WE GRIND OUR OWN
AND CURE OUR OWN
WE MAKE SYRUPS
LAURA, THANKS FOR MEETING WITH ME.
SURE. ARE YOU STILL WORKING ON DRONES? I'M LOOKING FOR NEW MATERIAL.
WHAT KIND OF MATERIAL? I HAVE SOME ACCESS TO WHISTLEBLOWERS AND TO VICTIMS.
THIS IS FOR AN ART EXHIBITION AT THE WHITNEY MUSEUM HERE IN NEW YORK. I'D LIKE PEOPLE TO EXPERIENCE THE WAR ITSELF.
THAT'S QUITE A TALL ORDER! WHAT DO YOU ENVISAGE?
AUDIO AND VIDEO FROM THE KILLING ZONE IF POSSIBLE.
I THINK REPRIEVE WOULD BE YOUR BEST BET FOR THAT.
MOON
I'VE BEEN TALKING TO THEM ABOUT A MEETING BETWEEN VICTIMS AND WHISTLEBLOWERS AND IT SEEMS THAT YOUR EXHIBITION COULD PROVIDE THE PERFECT OPPORTUNITY.
I THINK IT WOULD BE PRETTY HARD TO BRING DRONE VICTIMS TO THE UNITED STATES. I DOUBT THEY COULD GET VISAS. AND FROM WHAT YOU SAY, IT SOUNDS LIKE THE FORMER DRONE OPERATORS COULD BACK OUT AT THE LAST MOMENT.
ONCE AGAIN, I THINK THAT REPRIEVE CAN HELP. THEY HAVE CLIENTS IN BOTH PAKISTAN AND YEMEN WHO COULD TRY TO GET THE AUDIO AND VIDEO THAT YOU NEED.
ADAM
OK, LET'S GIVE IT A TRY.

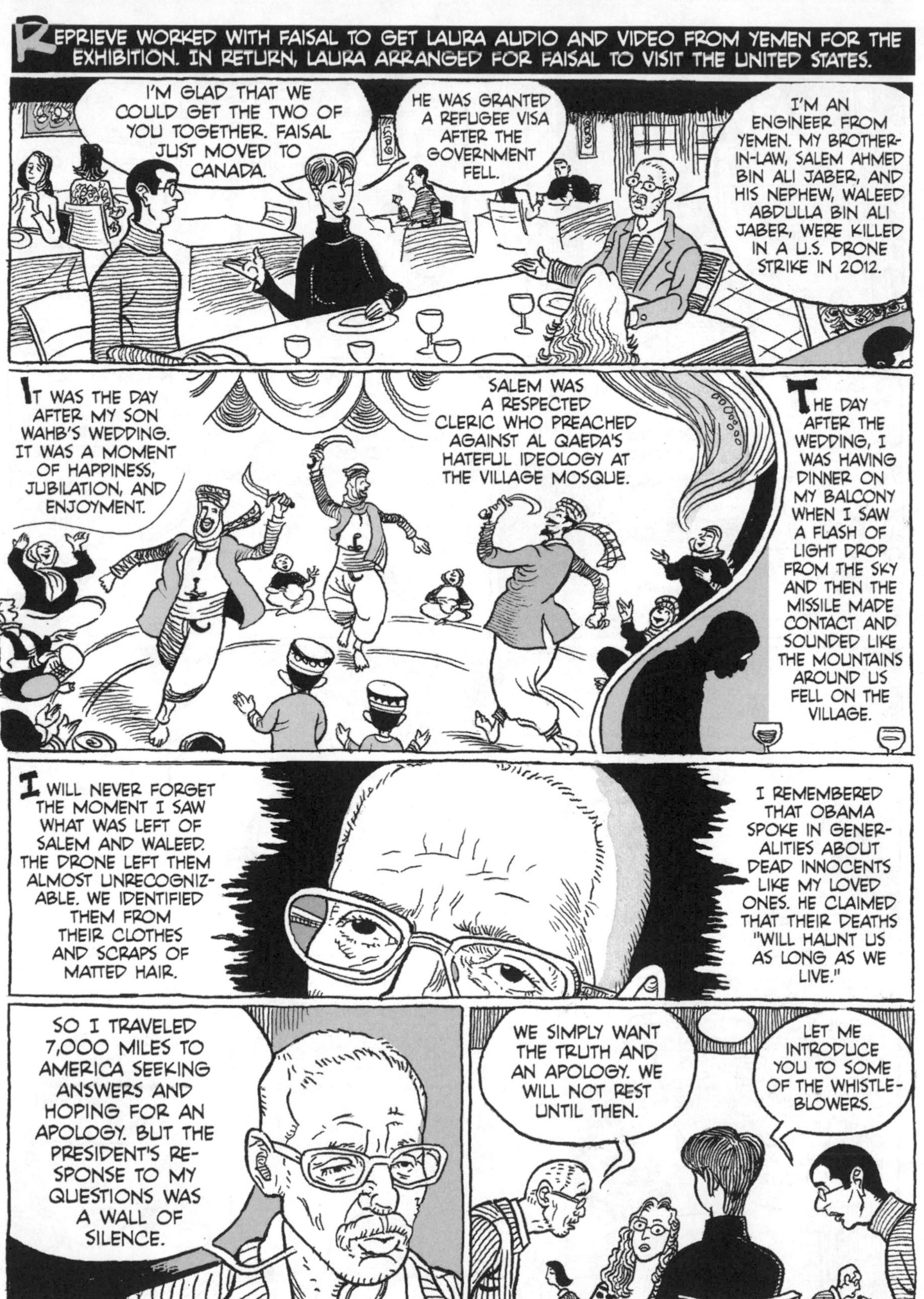
REPRIEVE WORKED WITH FAISAL TO GET LAURA AUDIO AND VIDEO FROM YEMEN FOR THE EXHIBITION. IN RETURN, LAURA ARRANGED FOR FAISAL TO VISIT THE UNITED STATES.
I'M GLAD THAT WE COULD GET THE TWO OF YOU TOGETHER. FAISAL JUST MOVED TO CANADA.
HE WAS GRANTED A REFUGEE VISA AFTER THE GOVERNMENT FELL.
I'M AN ENGINEER FROM YEMEN. MY BROTHER-IN-LAW, SALEM AHMED BIN ALI JABER, AND HIS NEPHEW, WALEED ABDULLA BIN ALI JABER, WERE KILLED IN A U.S. DRONE STRIKE IN 2012.
IT WAS THE DAY AFTER MY SON WAHB'S WEDDING. IT WAS A MOMENT OF HAPPINESS, JUBILATION, AND ENJOYMENT.
SALEM WAS A RESPECTED CLERIC WHO PREACHED AGAINST AL QAEDA'S HATEFUL IDEOLOGY AT THE VILLAGE MOSQUE.
THE DAY AFTER THE WEDDING, I WAS HAVING DINNER ON MY BALCONY WHEN I SAW A FLASH OF LIGHT DROP FROM THE SKY AND THEN THE MISSILE MADE CONTACT AND SOUNDED LIKE THE MOUNTAINS AROUND US FELL ON THE VILLAGE.
I WILL NEVER FORGET THE MOMENT I SAW WHAT WAS LEFT OF SALEM AND WALEED. THE DRONE LEFT THEM ALMOST UNRECOGNIZABLE. WE IDENTIFIED THEM FROM THEIR CLOTHES AND SCRAPS OF MATTED HAIR.
I REMEMBERED THAT OBAMA SPOKE IN GENERALITIES ABOUT DEAD INNOCENTS LIKE MY LOVED ONES. HE CLAIMED THAT THEIR DEATHS "WILL HAUNT US AS LONG AS WE LIVE."
SO I TRAVELED 7,000 MILES TO AMERICA SEEKING ANSWERS AND HOPING FOR AN APOLOGY. BUT THE PRESIDENT'S RESPONSE TO MY QUESTIONS WAS A WALL OF SILENCE.
WE SIMPLY WANT THE TRUTH AND AN APOLOGY. WE WILL NOT REST UNTIL THEN.
LET ME INTRODUCE YOU TO SOME OF THE WHISTLE-BLOWERS.

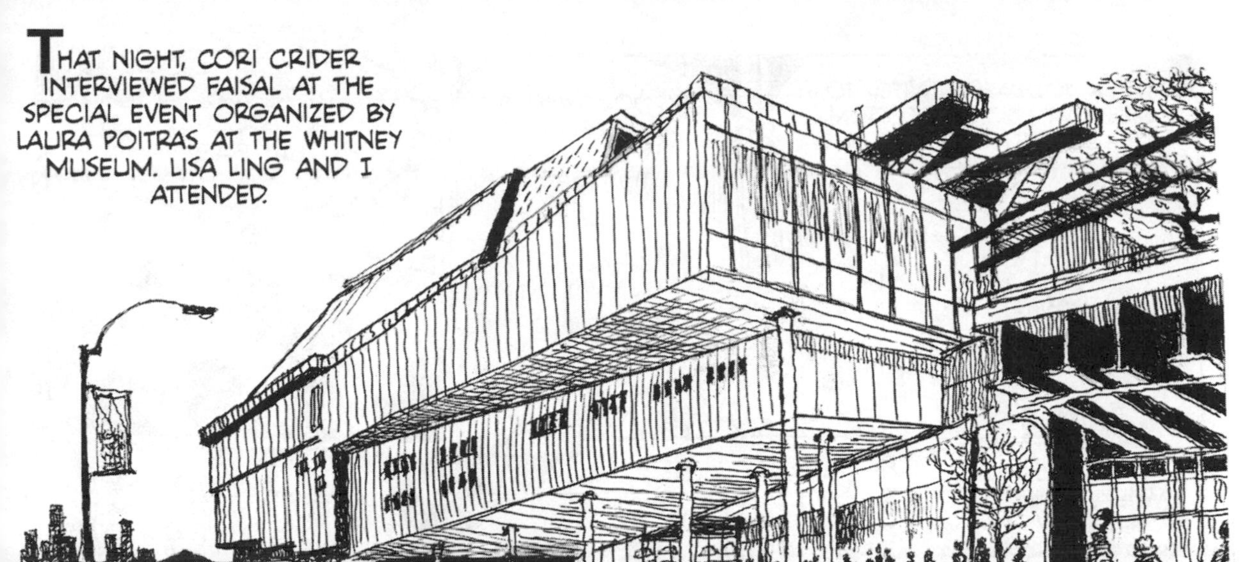
THAT NIGHT, CORI CRIDER INTERVIEWED FAISAL AT THE SPECIAL EVENT ORGANIZED BY LAURA POITRAS AT THE WHITNEY MUSEUM. LISA LING AND I ATTENDED.

LAURA POITRAS
ASTRO NOISE

FAISAL BIN ALI JABER

FAISAL, DID SOMEONE FROM THE YEMEN GOVERNMENT CONTACT YOU AFTER YOUR NEPHEW AND BROTHER-IN-LAW WERE KILLED?
YES, TWO OR THREE HOURS AFTER THE BOMBING.

SOMEONE CALLED FROM THE CAPITAL, SANA'A. HIS NAME WAS MUHAMMAD AND HE SAID HE WAS WITH THE ANTI-TERRORISM UNIT. HE SAID THAT SALEM AND WALEED WERE NOT THE TARGETS AND HE APOLOGIZED PROFUSELY.

I TOLD HIM THAT'S NOT ENOUGH AND WE NEED AN INVESTIGATION.

LATER YOU WERE INVITED TO MEET WITH SOMEONE FROM THE SECRET SERVICE. WHEN YOU WENT IN, THE MAN HELD OUT A PLASTIC BAG.
DO YOU WANT TO TELL EVERYBODY WHAT WAS IN THAT BAG?
THERE WAS $100,000 IN THAT BAG.
I KEPT ASKING WHERE DOES THE MONEY COME FROM, BUT THE MAN SAID THAT'S A SECRET.
I ASKED IF IT WAS FROM THE U.S. HE CONFIRMED VERBALLY.
BUT HE REFUSED TO PUT IT IN WRITING.
SO WHAT DID YOU DO WITH THE MONEY?
WE ARE HOLDING ON TO THE MONEY IN OUR QUEST FOR JUSTICE, FOR A PUBLIC APOLOGY.
CLAP
CLAP
CLAP
CLAP
CLAP
CLAP
CLAP
FAISAL, HOW HARD WAS IT FOR YOU TO ENTER THE UNITED STATES, GIVEN THAT THE GOVERNMENT WON'T MEET WITH YOU?
FAISAL HAS QUITE THE TALE TO TELL ABOUT THAT.
FAISAL, COULD YOU SHARE WHAT HAPPENED WHEN YOU ARRIVED AT JFK TWO NIGHTS AGO?
WELL, USUALLY I DON'T MIND THIS KIND OF IMMIGRATION PROCEDURE SINCE IT IS MEANT TO PROTECT US ALL.

BUT WHAT HAPPENED TWO NIGHTS AGO WITH THIS OFFICER WAS INTERESTING.

OK, WHY DON'T YOU TELL ME YOUR STORY THEN?
I TOLD THE OFFICER WHAT HAD HAPPENED TO MY BROTHER-IN-LAW AND NEPHEW AS HE WROTE DOWN THE NAME OF MY VILLAGE AND OTHER DETAILS.
AFTER A WHILE HE CAME BACK AND SHOOK MY HAND VERY WARMLY.
AND HE APOLOGIZED DEEPLY FOR WHAT HAD HAPPENED TO MY FAMILY.
HE EVEN INSISTED ON WALKING ME ALL THE WAY TO THE GATE.
CLAP CLAP CLAP CLAP CLAP CLAP CLAP
RIGHT AFTER THE Q AND A SESSION, LISA WENT UP TO MEET FAISAL.
MR. FAISAL, MY NAME IS LISA LING, AND I WORKED FOR THE U.S. MILITARY DRONE PROGRAM.
I WANT TO TELL YOU MY STORY AND TO APOLOGIZE FOR YOUR FAMILY'S SUFFERING.
AND I WANTED TO KNOW IF THERE IS ANYTHING I CAN DO TO HELP YOU IN YOUR CAUSE.

THE WHISTLEBLOWERS' LAWYERS HIT UPON AN IDEA TO HELP FAISAL OUT, BASED ON THE CASE OF WEINSTEIN AND LO PORTO, REMEMBER THEM?
YES, THE ONLY TWO DRONE VICTIMS WHOSE DEATHS OBAMA APOLOGIZED FOR.
WELL, BEFORE OBAMA LEFT OFFICE HE AGREED TO PAY COMPENSATION TO LO PORTO'S FAMILY.
LO PORTO
WEINSTEIN
AN ITALIAN LAWYER BY THE NAME OF GIULIA BORGNA NEGOTIATED A DEAL WITH THE U.S. EMBASSY IN ROME.
La Repubblica
by Stefania Maurizi
U.S. TO PAY €1.2 MILLION TO LO PORTO FAMILY!
WOW, THAT'S ABOUT $1.3 MILLION IN U.S. DOLLARS! FAISAL GOT $100,000.
ONE ITALIAN EQUALS 13 YEMENIS?
THE OBAMA ADMINISTRATION ALSO ISSUED A DOCUMENT SAYING THAT THEY KILLED BETWEEN 64 AND 116 PEOPLE BY MISTAKE.
ANY APOLOGIES?
THEY DIDN'T EVEN HOLD A PRESS CONFERENCE, LET ALONE APOLOGIZE. THEY JUST PUBLISHED THE INFORMATION ON A FRIDAY AFTERNOON RIGHT BEFORE EVERYONE LEFT ON HOLIDAY FOR INDEPENDENCE DAY SO THAT IT WOULD GET AS LITTLE MEDIA AS POSSIBLE.
AND THE ONLY REASON THEY EVEN PUBLISHED THE DATA WAS BECAUSE THE ACLU SUED THEM FOR IT.
DID THEY NAME THE PEOPLE THAT THEY KILLED?
NOPE. THEY DIDN'T EVEN SAY WHICH COUNTRIES THESE PEOPLE WERE KILLED IN.

WHY CAN'T NON-WESTERNERS GET APOLOGIES, TOO?
THAT'S EXACTLY WHAT REPRIEVE HAS BEEN DEMANDING.
JENNIFER GIBSON, REPRIEVE
DEMOCRACY NOW!
WHY WON'T THE U.S. GOVERNMENT COME CLEAN AND APOLOGIZE TO **ALL** THE CIVILIANS KILLED BY THE MISGUIDED DRONE PROGRAMS?
DEMOCRACY NOW!
THE LO PORTO FAMILY'S TERRIBLE ORDEAL SHOWS THAT THE SECRET DRONE PROGRAM IS NOTHING LIKE AS ACCURATE AS THE U.S. GOVERNMENT CLAIMS.
REPRIEVE FILED A LAWSUIT ASKING THE WHITE HOUSE TO MAKE A PERSONAL APOLOGY TO FAISAL AND TO ADMIT THAT HIS RELATIVES WERE INNOCENT.
UNITED STATES COURTS ★ D.C. ★ OF COLUMBIA
BRANDON, CIAN, AND LISA SUBMITTED A STATEMENT TO THE COURT IN SUPPORT OF FAISAL'S REQUEST.
REPRIEVE,
Petition.
Respondents
BRIEF FOR
AMICUS CURIAE, SERVING IN THE
AIR FORCE, AMICI WITNESSED
WIDESPREAD AND DELIBERATE
MISCLASSIFICATION OF DEATHS
LISA LING HEATHER
CIAN WESTMORELAND
Counsel for Amicus
LISA LING
FAISAL DESERVES THE TRUTH!
CIAN WEST-MORELAND
PEOPLE HAVE THE RIGHT TO KNOW HOW A SCREW-UP CAN LEAD TO THE DEATH OF THEIR FAMILY MEMBERS. THIS IS ABOUT ACCOUNTABILITY, TRANSPARENCY, AND HOW WE CAN LEARN FROM OUR MISTAKES.

Chapter Sixteen

NEW YORK CITY
ELECTION NIGHT, NOVEMBER 8, 2016.
DONALD TRUMP DEFEATED HILLARY CLINTON IN A STUNNING UPSET THAT FEW POLITICAL PUNDITS EXPECTED, THROWING THE COUNTRY AND WASHINGTON INTO TURMOIL.
TRUMP
PENCE
MAKE AMERICA GREAT AGAIN
MAKE AMERICA GREAT
TRUMP TRIUMPHS
OUTSIDER MOGUL CAPTURES PRESIDENCY
Liberation
EDITION SPECIALE
TRUMP APOCALYPSE
IT'S TRUMP
WHAT WILL THIS MEAN FOR THE NATIONAL SECURITY STATE?
WE WILL ERADICATE RADICAL ISLAMIC TERRORISM COMPLETELY FROM THE FACE OF THE EARTH.
Daily Telegraph
God Save America
WILL TRUMP RAMP UP THE WAR ON TERROR?
SCALE IT DOWN?
NOBODY KNOWS.
TRUMP
PENCE
MAKE AMERICA GREAT AGAIN

GLENN GREENWALD CAPTURED THE DEEP IRONY OF THE MOMENT IN AN OP-ED FOR THE *WASHINGTON POST*.

TRUMP WILL COMMAND... THE ABILITY TO WAGE NUMEROUS WARS IN SECRET AND WITHOUT CONGRESSIONAL AUTHORIZATION; A UBIQUITOUS SYSTEM OF ELECTRONIC SURVEILLANCE...

AND COUNTLESS METHODS FOR SHIELDING HIMSELF FROM JUDICIAL ACCOUNTABILITY, CONGRESSIONAL OVERSIGHT AND THE RULE OF LAW... OBAMA NOT ONLY CONTINUED MANY OF THE MOST EXTREME EXECUTIVE-POWER POLICIES HE ONCE CONDEMNED, BUT... STRENGTHENED AND EXTENDED THEM. HIS ADMINISTRATION DETAINED TERRORISM SUSPECTS WITHOUT DUE PROCESS...

...PROPOSED NEW FRAMEWORKS TO KEEP THEM LOCKED UP WITHOUT TRIAL, TARGETED THOUSANDS... FOR EXECUTION BY DRONE, AND COVERTLY EXPANDED THE NATION'S MASS ELECTRONIC SURVEILLANCE...

THIS IS THE UNRESTRAINED SET OF POWERS TRUMP WILL INHERIT... THE DEMOCRATS ARE NOW ALARMED... BUT IF THEY WANT TO KNOW WHOM TO BLAME, THEY SHOULD LOOK IN THE MIRROR...

THAT DAY HAS ARRIVED.

CIVIL LIBERTIES ADVOCATES... TRIED... TO PERSUADE AND CAJOLE DEMOCRATS... DEMOCRATS WERE URGED, TO IMAGINE THAT A RIGHT-WING AUTHORITARIAN, OR A LAWLESS DEMAGOGUE, WON THE PRESIDENCY AND INHERITED THE FRAMEWORK OF UNRESTRAINED, UNCHECKED POWERS...

I CALLED CIAN AND LISA TO SEE IF THE ELECTION WOULD CAUSE THEM TO RECONSIDER THEIR WORK

MY WORST FEARS ABOUT TRUMP'S POLICIES IMMEDIATELY CAME TRUE.
YAKLA, YEMEN, JANUARY 22, 2017
CREECH AIR FORCE BASE.
BARAA SHIBAN, YEMENI FELLOW FOR REPRIEVE
PEOPLE WERE AFRAID TO LEAVE THEIR HOUSES BECAUSE THE SOUND OF CHOPPERS AND DRONES WERE ALL OVER THE SKY.
THEY WERE JUST FARMERS WHO WERE WORKING DURING THE DAY.
EVERYONE FEARED BEING HIT BY THE DRONES...
...OR SHOT BY THE SOLDIERS ON THE GROUND.
AL-JAZEERA EXCLUSIVE
AT TWO IN THE MORNING, AMERICAN PLANES STRUCK OUR TOWN AND KILLED INNOCENT CIVILIANS.
WHOLE FAMILIES WERE WIPED OUT WITH APACHES AND DRONES.
ALJAZEERA
AL-JAZEERA
THE ATTACK WAS THE FIRST MILITARY OPERATION AUTHORIZED BY PRESIDENT DONALD TRUMP.

IT DIDN'T GO AS PLANNED...

THE RAID TARGETED THE HOUSE OF A TRIBAL LEADER ABDULRAOUR AL-DHAHAB. THE U.S. SUSPECTS HE WAS A SENIOR AL QAEDA COMMANDER, BUT LOCALS SAY THAT'S NOT TRUE.

ONE OF HIS BROTHERS WAS ASSOCIATED WITH AL QAEDA, BUT HE WAS KILLED A WHILE BACK.

RESIDENTS SAY THAT AT LEAST EIGHT WOMEN AND SEVEN CHILDREN WERE KILLED.

OBAMA KILLED A 16-YEAR-OLD AMERICAN IN YEMEN. TRUMP JUST KILLED HIS 8-YEAR-OLD SISTER.

REUTERS

WORLD NEWS/Thu March 2, 2017
Strike in Kuram, Pakistan, 2 killed.

REUTERS

WORLD NEWS/Fri March 3 , 2017
Strike in Yasham Valley, Yemen. 1-8 killed. Possible civilian casualties.

WORLD NEWS/Thu March 6, 2017
Strike in Abyan Province, Yemen. 11 reported killed, 2 children reported dead

MICAH ZENKO, COUNCIL ON FOREIGN RELATIONS

DURING PRESIDENT OBAMA'S TWO TERMS IN OFFICE, HE APPROVED 542 SUCH TARGETED ATTACKS IN 2,920 DAYS — ONE EVERY 5.4 DAYS. FROM HIS INAUGURATION THROUGH TODAY, PRESIDENT TRUMP HAD APPROVED AT LEAST 75 DRONE STRIKES OR RAIDS IN 74 DAYS — ABOUT ONE IN EVERY 1.25 DAYS.

THE FAULT LIES WITH THE INTELLIGENCE AGENCIES AND THE MILITARY, WHO ROUTINELY FAIL AT THEIR TASKS. THIS HAPPENS ALL THE TIME.
THE DATA THEY COLLECT IS OFTEN WRONG. THE ANALYSIS THEY PRODUCE IS OFTEN TERRIBLE, BUT IT IS RARELY MADE PUBLIC. EVERY SO OFTEN WE GET A GLIMPSE OF THIS.
REMEMBER HOW OBAMA FORCED DOWN THE PLANE OF THE BOLIVIAN PRESIDENT UNDER THE FALSE MPRESSION THAT SNOWDEN HAD STOWED AWAY?
AND WHO CAN FORGET HOW THEY HARASSED LAURA POITRAS EVERY TIME SHE ENTERED THE UNITED STATES, WHEN IT TURNED OUT...
...SHE WAS MISTAKENLY PUT ON THE NO-FLY LIST JUST FOR BEING PRESENT AT A CERTAIN SITE IN BAGHDAD THE DAY BEFORE A U.S. SOLDIER WAS KILLED AT THE SAME SPOT.
AND HOW ABOUT THE INFAMOUS WARRANT ISSUED FOR EDWARD JAMES SNOWDEN IN HONG KONG, INSTEAD OF EDWARD JOSEPH SNOWDEN?
A NO-FLY LIST FEATURING TENS OF THOUSANDS OF OTHERS, INCLUDING MEMBERS OF THE U.S. CONGRESS, LIKE SENATOR TED KENNEDY AND CONGRESSMAN JOHN LEWIS!
WHEN IT COMES TO DRONES, THESE KINDS OF ERRORS KILL INNOCENT PEOPLE. BUT THERE'S A PATTERN TO THE THE ERRORS THAT SHOWS THIS IS MORE THAN JUST INCOMPETENCE AND BAD DATA.
I'VE BEEN TALKING TO PHILIP GARNETT, A MATHEMATICIAN AT THE UNIVERSITY OF YORK IN ENGLAND.
HE'S BEEN STUDYING THE ALGORITHMS THAT DRONES USE.

Chapter Seventeen

direction
magnitude

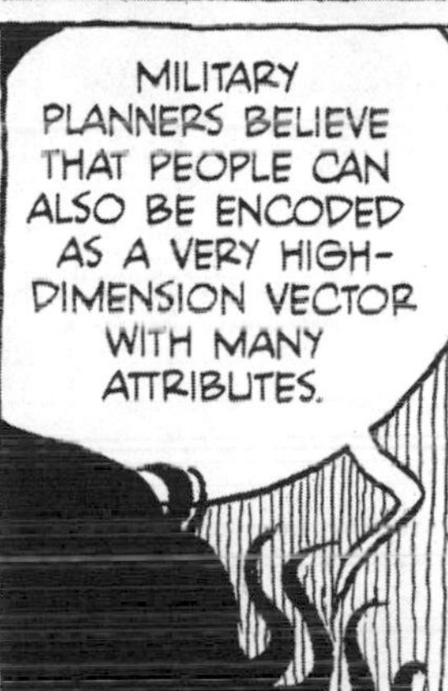

Vectorising the Human

Altitudinal
- Preferences
- Price sensitivity
- Loyalty

Demographic
- Age
- Income
- Marital status
- Kids?
- Education
- Gender

Behavioral
- Buying habits
- How you pay
- Price paid

Lifestyle
- Internet use
- Car?
- Travel
- Hobbies

NEXT, THEY USE ALGORITHMS, THAT IS TO SAY MATHEMATICAL RULES TO TRY TO IDENTIFY TERRORISTS

FROM NON-TERRORISTS. BUT SO MANY HUMAN DATA ATTRIBUTES ARE HARD TO ENCODE. NO TWO PEOPLE ARE THE SAME EVEN IF ALL THEIR ATTRIBUTES ARE THE SAME.

IN TERMS OF ATTRIBUTES, THE DIFFERENCE BETWEEN NON-EXTREMISTS AND EXTREMISTS CAN BE VERY SMALL.

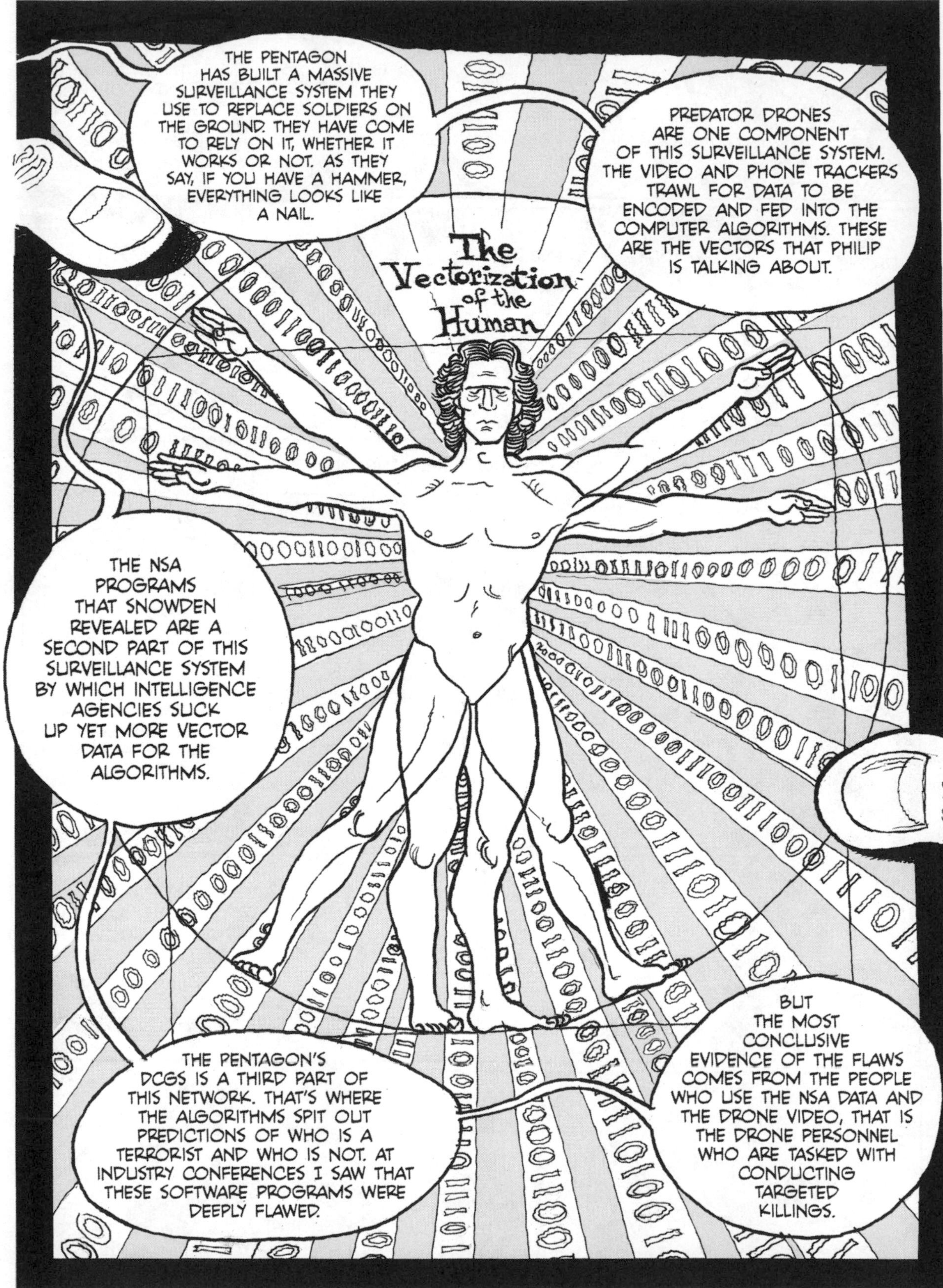
THE PENTAGON HAS BUILT A MASSIVE SURVEILLANCE SYSTEM THEY USE TO REPLACE SOLDIERS ON THE GROUND. THEY HAVE COME TO RELY ON IT, WHETHER IT WORKS OR NOT. AS THEY SAY, IF YOU HAVE A HAMMER, EVERYTHING LOOKS LIKE A NAIL.
PREDATOR DRONES ARE ONE COMPONENT OF THIS SURVEILLANCE SYSTEM. THE VIDEO AND PHONE TRACKERS TRAWL FOR DATA TO BE ENCODED AND FED INTO THE COMPUTER ALGORITHMS. THESE ARE THE VECTORS THAT PHILIP IS TALKING ABOUT.
The Vectorization of the Human
THE NSA PROGRAMS THAT SNOWDEN REVEALED ARE A SECOND PART OF THIS SURVEILLANCE SYSTEM BY WHICH INTELLIGENCE AGENCIES SUCK UP YET MORE VECTOR DATA FOR THE ALGORITHMS.
THE PENTAGON'S DCGS IS A THIRD PART OF THIS NETWORK. THAT'S WHERE THE ALGORITHMS SPIT OUT PREDICTIONS OF WHO IS A TERRORIST AND WHO IS NOT. AT INDUSTRY CONFERENCES I SAW THAT THESE SOFTWARE PROGRAMS WERE DEEPLY FLAWED.
BUT THE MOST CONCLUSIVE EVIDENCE OF THE FLAWS COMES FROM THE PEOPLE WHO USE THE NSA DATA AND THE DRONE VIDEO, THAT IS THE DRONE PERSONNEL WHO ARE TASKED WITH CONDUCTING TARGETED KILLINGS.

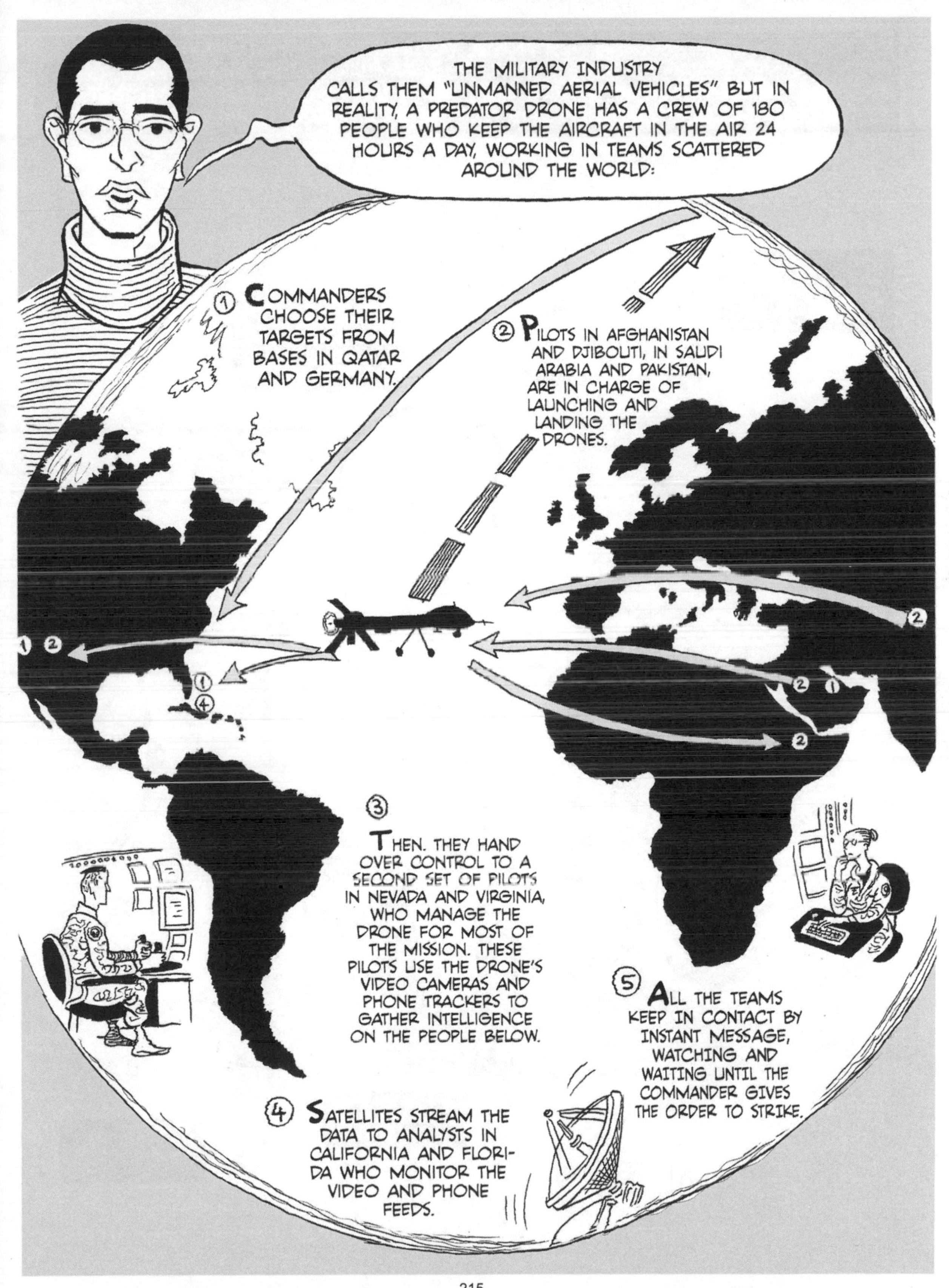
THE MILITARY INDUSTRY CALLS THEM "UNMANNED AERIAL VEHICLES" BUT IN REALITY, A PREDATOR DRONE HAS A CREW OF 180 PEOPLE WHO KEEP THE AIRCRAFT IN THE AIR 24 HOURS A DAY, WORKING IN TEAMS SCATTERED AROUND THE WORLD:
1 COMMANDERS CHOOSE THEIR TARGETS FROM BASES IN QATAR AND GERMANY.
2 PILOTS IN AFGHANISTAN AND DJIBOUTI, IN SAUDI ARABIA AND PAKISTAN, ARE IN CHARGE OF LAUNCHING AND LANDING THE DRONES.
3 THEN. THEY HAND OVER CONTROL TO A SECOND SET OF PILOTS IN NEVADA AND VIRGINIA, WHO MANAGE THE DRONE FOR MOST OF THE MISSION. THESE PILOTS USE THE DRONE'S VIDEO CAMERAS AND PHONE TRACKERS TO GATHER INTELLIGENCE ON THE PEOPLE BELOW.
4 SATELLITES STREAM THE DATA TO ANALYSTS IN CALIFORNIA AND FLORIDA WHO MONITOR THE VIDEO AND PHONE FEEDS.
5 ALL THE TEAMS KEEP IN CONTACT BY INSTANT MESSAGE, WATCHING AND WAITING UNTIL THE COMMANDER GIVES THE ORDER TO STRIKE.

THE TRUTH IS THAT THESE SOLDIERS MUST ANALYZE VAST AMOUNTS OF VIDEO, PHONE CALLS AND SOCIAL MEDIA DATA - ALL FROM A COMPLETELY UNFAMILIAR CULTURE, IN A DIFFERENT LANGUAGE. LIKE THE PROVERBIAL ELEPHANT WHOSE ENTIRE LIKENESS CANNOT BE GRASPED BY BLINDFOLDED OBSERVERS, THE TRUE IDENTITY OF A POTENTIAL DRONE TARGET OFTEN REMAINS ELUSIVE.

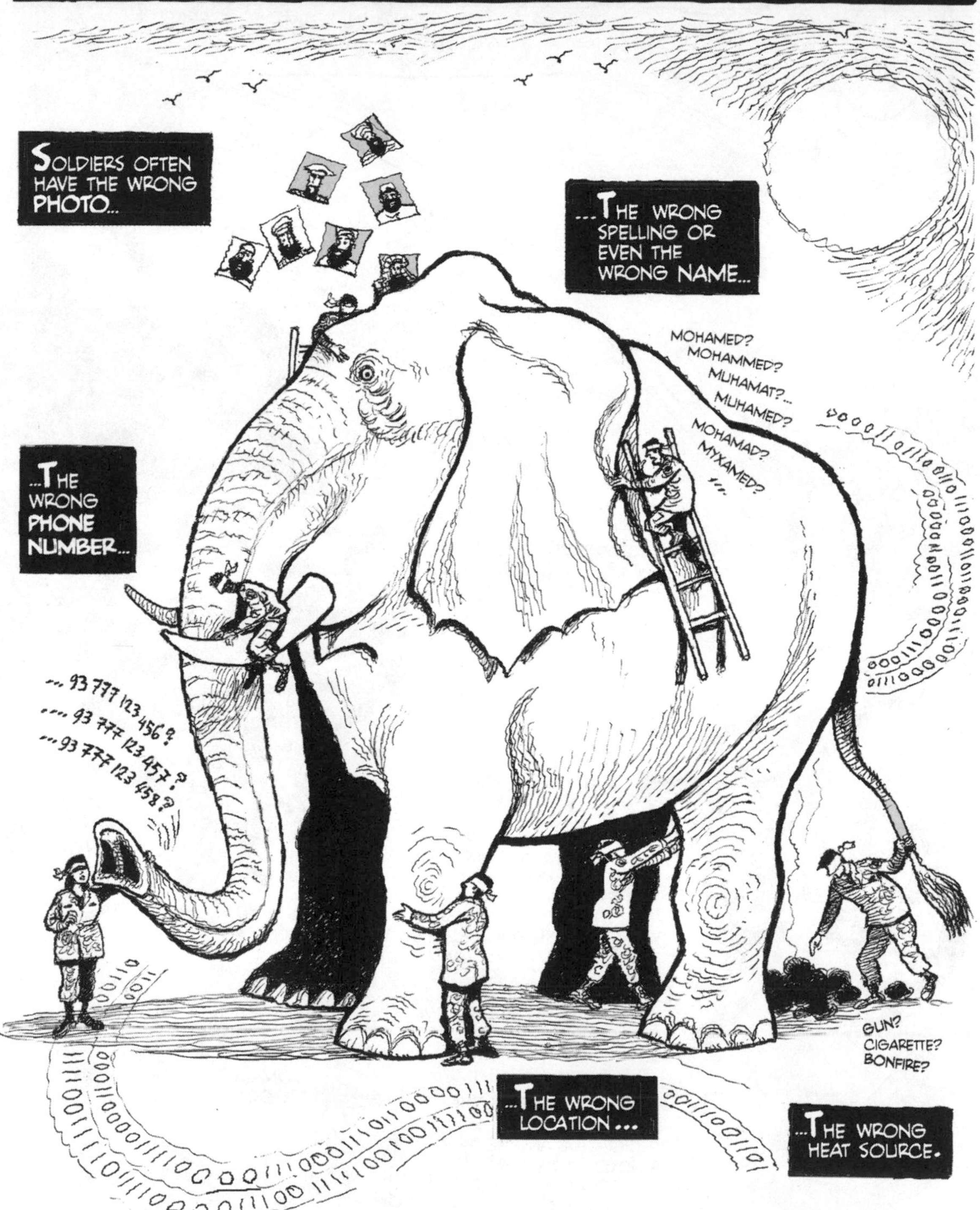

IN HOLLYWOOD MOVIES, DRONE PILOTS CAN SEE IN HIGH DEFINITION.
THEY CAN WATCH THEIR TARGET DAY AND NIGHT...
...FOLLOW THEM THROUGH BUILDINGS...
...SEE THEIR FACES...
...AND SPOT A TREMBLING FINGER ON A TRIGGER.
IN REAL LIFE, IT'S EASY TO MAKE MISTAKES. WHEN I WAS ASKED TO IDENTIFY TARIQ, THE TEENAGER FROM WAZIRISTAN, AFTER HE WAS KILLED BY A CIA DRONE, I PICKED THE WRONG PHOTO, NOT REALIZING THAT THERE WERE TWO BOYS NAMED TARIQ SITTING RIGHT NEXT TO EACH OTHER.
ACCORDING TO FORMER BBC REPORTER, KATE CLARKE, THE KILLING OF ZABET AMINULLAH IN AFGHANISTAN OCCURED BECAUSE THE MILITARY HAD THE WRONG PHONE NUMBER.
I IMAGINE THEY KILLED FAISAL BIN JABER'S RELATIVES FOR THE SAME REASON: THEY HAD THE WRONG NAME OR NUMBER.
AND VIDEO FROM DRONES CAN'T DISTINGUISH BETWEEN MEN AND WOMEN AND CHILDREN: THAT IS WHY 23 INNOCENT VILLAGERS WERE KILLED IN URUZGAN.
IN REALITY, JUST AS WE CAN ONLY SEE ONE SCENE THROUGH A PAIR OF BINOCULARS, A PREDATOR OPERATOR CAN ONLY WATCH ONE PERSON AT A TIME. THEY CALL IT THE "SODA STRAW VIEW."

THE MILITARY KNOWS 19-YEAR-OLDS LIKE BRANDON, CIAN, AND HEATHER CAN'T PINPOINT TARGETS ON THEIR OWN. INSTEAD DCGS CALCULATES IT FOR THEM.
IT'S A SYSTEM THAT THE PENTAGON CALLS "CROSS SENSOR CUEING."
U2 RECONNAISSANCE AIRCRAFT
FOR INSTANCE, WHEN A PHONE SIGNAL FROM A WANTED TARGET IS PICKED UP BY A U2 RECONNAISSANCE AIRCRAFT 60,000 FEET ABOVE SYRIA, DCGS IS ALERTED IN VIRGINIA...
NRO SATELLITE
U2 PILOT 60,000 FEET
...WHICH AUTOMATICALLY INSTRUCTS THE PILOT IN NEVADA TO FLY A PREDATOR IN FOR A CLOSER LOOK FROM 10,000 FEET AND POTENTIALLY FIRE A MISSILE.
DCGS OPERATOR, LANGLEY, VIRGINIA
DRONE OPERATOR CREECH, NEVADA
DRONE 10,000 FT
TARGET PHONE, SYRIA
IMAGERY ANALYST, HURLBURT FIELD, FLA
DESPITE BEING HALF-WAY ACROSS THE WORLD, THANKS TO THE GLOBAL COMPUTER NETWORK, THESE PILOTS ARE ABLE TO FLY DRONES, WATCH TARGETS, AND THEN KILL THEM FROM AFAR.

THE MILITARY CALLS THIS PROCESS SHORTENING THE SENSOR TO SHOOTER TIMELINE.
ESSENTIALLY, IF YOU SEE SOMTHING, DO SOMETHING.
I HAVE PROOF THAT THE PENTAGON KNOWS THAT THE DCGS PHONE LOCATION SYSTEM DOESN'T WORK..
The median differences in ground truth and reported locations were between one and two kilometers. Only 10 in 41 test records provided contain info to compare descriptions and locations of the wanted targets.
AN ARMY EVALUATION FROM JANUARY 2016
AND HERE IS AN AIR FORCE EVALUATION FROM JULY 2016.
"SYSTEM WAS ONLY UP AND WORKING 33 PERCENT OF THE TIME."
AF-DCGS
33 Percent
WHY DOES THE PENTAGON TRUST THIS SOFTWARE, THEN?
MAGICAL THINKING. IT'S MUCH EASIER TO TRUST A MACHINE, WHEN THE ALTERNATIVE IS A TEENAGER WHO DOES NOT SPEAK THE LANGUAGE OR KNOW THE CULTURE.
AND THE ARMS INDUSTRY IS HAPPY TO SELL SOFTWARE PROMISING THE ABILITY TO WIN A WAR FROM THE COMFORT OF A DESKTOP ON THE OTHER SIDE OF THE WORLD...
...WITHOUT EVER PUTTING BOOTS ON THE GROUND.
WHO MAKES THIS SOFTWARE?
THAT'S SOMETHING I HAVE BEEN RESEARCHING SINCE WIKILEAKS FIRST SHARED INFORMATION ABOUT THE SURVEILLANCE COMPANIES IN 2011.
YOU MEAN THE BROCHURES THAT GOT YOU FIRED?

THERE ISN'T ONE SINGLE SOFTWARE COMPANY: DCGS ITSELF HAS OVER SEVENTY VENDORS BUILDING DIFFERENT COMPONENTS...
NRO
NORTHROP-GRUMMAN
DIA
GENERAL ATOMICS
TICOM GEOMATICS
L-3 COMMUNICATIONS
Mediterranean Sea
AVIATION UNMANNED
CACI
ADVANCED CONCEPTS ENTERPRISES
NETEZZA
GENERAL DYNAMICS
INTREPID SOLUTIONS
BAE SYSTEMS
MACAULEY-BROWN
SAIC
BOOZ ALLEN HAMILTON
TRANS-VOYANT
WORLDWIDE LANGUAGE RESOURCES
SIX THREE
ZEL TECHNOLOGIES
CIA
Red Sea
NSA

...PERFORMING ALL SORTS OF COORDINATED, COMPLIMENTARY TASKS.
NGA
DHS
RAYTHEON
FBI
Indian Ocean
SOME OF THE TASKS:
1. LAUNCH AND RECOVERY; MISSION CONTROL; SAFETY OBSERVERS; PILOTS.
2. GYROSCOPES, GIMBALS, AND INERTIAL MEASUREMENT UNITS.
3. FULL MOTION VIDEO.
4. THERMAL AND INFRARED IMAGERY.
5. SYNTHETIC APERTURE RADAR.
6. GEOLOCATION AND PHONE TRACKING.
7. LINGUISTS AND JUDGE ADVOCATE GENERALS.
8. BIG DATA AND SOCIAL NETWORK ANALYSIS.
9. DISTRIBUTED COMMON GROUND SYSTEM.
10. NETWORK-CENTRIC COLLABORATIVE TARGETING SYSTEM.

YOUR LIST OF COMPANIES READS LIKE A REGULAR WHO'S WHO OF THE INFAMOUS MILITARY-INDUSTRIAL COMPLEX THAT EISENHOWER WARNED US ABOUT UPON LEAVING OFFICE.

THE FIRST — AND LAST — U.S. PRESIDENT TO EVER MENTION THE ELEPHANT IN THE ROOM.

Epilogue

FOUR YEARS AFTER EDWARD SNOWDEN REVEALED THE HORRIFYING EXTENT OF GOVERNMENT SURVEILLANCE...

...PRESERVING PRIVACY HAS BECOME A TOP AGENDA ITEM FOR DATA PROVIDERS AND LAW MAKERS.

MULTIPLE PUBLIC HEARINGS HAVE BEEN HELD TO INVESTIGATE ABUSE BY THE INTELLIGENCE AGENCIES.

THE USA FREEDOM ACT OF 2015 HAS AMENDED PART OF THE CONTROVERSIAL PATRIOT ACT.* TELECOM COMPANIES CAN NO LONGER BE FORCED TO TURN OVER BULK PHONE RECORDS...

...ALTHOUGH THE GOVERNMENT CAN **STILL** ASK THEM FOR DATA ON SPECIFIC USERS.

PUBLIC SUPPORT FOR WHISTLEBLOWERS HAS SKYROCKETED, DESPITE DRACONIAN CRACKDOWNS BY WASHINGTON.

WIKILEAKS HAS PUBLISHED EVIDENCE THAT THE CIA AND NSA ARE DESIGNING NEW AND EVEN MORE INVASIVE SOFTWARE TOOLS...

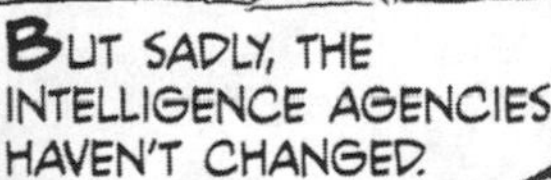

BUT SADLY, THE INTELLIGENCE AGENCIES HAVEN'T CHANGED.

...THAT INVITE MISUSE AND SURVEILLANCE OF CIVILIANS, LIKE **WEEPING ANGEL** TO ATTACK SMART TVS; **AFTER-MIDNIGHT** AND **ASSASSIN** TO COMPROMISE WINDOWS USERS. ALSO, THE NSA FAILED TO TELL MICROSOFT ABOUT THE **WANNACRY** SOFTWARE FLAW, ALLOWING CYBER-CRIMINALS TO ATTACK FEDEX, BRITAIN'S NATIONAL HEALTH SERVICE, AND DEUTSCHE BAHN IN GERMANY.

TAKEN TOGETHER, THESE VAST POWERS CAN CONFER GOD-LIKE OMNISCIENCE ON WHOEVER HAS CONTROL OVER THEM. IN THE HANDS OF A VENGEFUL, IDEOLOGICAL, OR IRRATIONAL PERSON...

*SIGNED INTO LAW IN 2001, GIVING GOVERNMENT VAST SURVEILLANCE POWERS.

...WHO KNOWS HOW THESE POWERFUL WEAPONS COULD BE USED AGAINST US?
WHAT IF A ROGUE GOVERNMENT OFFICIAL SHUT DOWN THE BANKING SYSTEM, AIR TRAFFIC, AND THE ELECTRIC GRID?
BANK
WHAT IF CYBER-CRIMINALS SEIZED THESE WEAPONS AND USED THEM TO BLOW UP NUCLEAR REACTORS?
OR IF DISSIDENTS WERE HUNTED AND ASSASSINATED?

U.S. AIR FORCE
Creech Air Force Base
Indian Springs, Nevada
AND WHAT IF OUR SYSTEMS ARE WRONG?
HEY, YOU CAN TRUST ODIN AND GILGAMESH!
WITH HIS ONE EYE, ODIN CAN SEE MORE THAN ALL THE JIHADIS IN THE MIDDLE EAST COMBINED!
AND GILGAMESH IS NO SLOUCH, EITHER!

WE'RE AT WAR WITH MILITANT ISLAM! DO WE HAVE TO ALWAYS BE RIGHT?

WE DON'T TAKE STRIKES TO PUNISH INDIVIDUALS, WE ACT AGAINST TERRORISTS THREATENING AMERICA!

BUT IF WE KILL INNOCENT PEOPLE, WHAT ABOUT BLOW-BACK?

YOU AND I BOTH KNOW THE DATA ISN'T ALWAYS ACCURATE. EVEN GOOD INTEL ISN'T THE SAME AS EVIDENCE.
WE'RE THE ONLY ONES WHO CAN STOP THIS CARNAGE BY SPEAKING UP.

REMEMBER BRADLEY MANNING, THE SOLDIER WHO WAS JAILED FOR BLOWING THE WHISTLE IN IRAQ?
THE GUY WHO BECAME A WOMAN?

YEAH, YOU KNOW WHAT SHE SAID?

"WE'RE GETTING ALL THIS INFORMATION FROM ALL THESE DIFFERENT SOURCES AND IT'S JUST DEATH, DESTRUCTION, MAYHEM.
WE'RE FILTERING ALL THROUGH FACTS, STATISTICS, REPORTS, DATES, TIMES, LOCATIONS, AND EVENTUALLY JUST STOP. I STOPPED SEEING JUST STATISITCS AND INFORMATION AND I JUST STARTED SEEING **PEOPLE**.
I HAVE A RESPONSIBILITY TO THE PUBLIC... WE ALL HAVE A RESPONSIBILITY."
— CHELSEA MANNING

ACKNOWLEDGMENTS

The authors would like to thank Riva Hocherman at Metropolitan Books for her careful and brilliant editing; Sam Stoloff, our agent, for his patient and unstinting help; and our families, notably Song Chin-Bendib, Lily Smith, and Kiran Chatterjee for all their support during countless long days and nights of work. Special thanks to Connor Guy and Kelly Too at Metropolitan, and to Victor Lee and Kelly Oden, our interns, for saving us from missing almost all our deadlines.

We would also like to thank the staff of the Bureau of Investigative Journalism, Reprieve, and the Whistleblower and Source Protection Program at ExposeFacts. Last but of course not least, we would like to thank all the whistleblowers who came forward to speak out, despite the threat to their own careers and lives.

ABOUT THE AUTHORS

PRATAP CHATTERJEE is the author of *Halliburton's Army* and *Iraq, Inc.* The executive director of Corpwatch, he has written for publications including *The New Republic,* the *Financial Times*, and *The Guardian.* He has also won awards from the Overseas Club of America and the International consortium of Investigative Journalists.

KHALIL (KHALIL BENDIB) is the co-author of the *New York Times* bestseller *Zahra's Paradise,* which was published in sixteen languages and nominated for two Eisner Awards. He also received the James Aronson Award for Journalism. His political cartoons are distributed to 1,700 publications nationwide.